SORELLA

EMMA HEARST & SARAH KRATHEN

PHOTOGRAPHS BY ANAIS & DAX

OLIVE PRESS

Olive Press

Recipes and text © 2013 by Emma Hearst and Sarah Krathen

Images © Anais & Dax

All rights reserved, including the right of reproduction
in whole or in part in any form

Olive Press is an imprint of Weldon Owen, Inc. and Williams-Sonoma, Inc.

Weldon Owen, Inc. is a division of Bonnier Corporation

415 Jackson Street, Suite 200, San Francisco, CA 94111

Library of Congress Control Number 2013945054

ISBN 978-1-61628-604-0

www.weldonowen.com

www.williams-sonoma.com

Printed and bound in China by Toppan-Leefung

First printed in 2013

10 9 8 7 6 5 4 3 2 1

SORELLA
MEANS SISTER

Sorella, which means "sister" in Italian, is the name of our New York City restaurant. Although we are not sisters by blood, we are by friendship. And we share the intimate details of our bond daily with our guests through our food, our hospitality, and the many inside jokes carefully placed throughout the restaurant.

We come from very different places, but we grew up together in Sorella. We signed away our twenties and learned life lessons and maturity the hard way, by building and running a restaurant. Travel provided us with the inspiration to help finalize our concept. But what we really fell in love with in Italy was the importance of family and tradition.

Here in New York City, a place that's home to some of the best food in the world, we aspire to transport our guests to contemporary Piedmont. We genuinely love what we do, and despite our age, we strive to cook like little old Italian grandmothers. We want our guests to feel comfortable and spoiled when they are with us. And when they leave us, they should feel as if they are leaving an Italian grandmother's house, with red cheeks not from pinching but from the warmth of memorable food and drink. We are wildly happy to be extending our reach by sharing our recipes and stories with a larger family. We hope you will enjoy what you find in these pages, and we encourage you to be adventurous. Keep in mind that what may seem weird at first is surely delicious. And, yes, we are talking about the food.

Ciao,

Emma + Sarah

ON HOSPITALITY

At Sorella, we refer to ourselves as hospitalians. The name does double duty, even though we are not actually Italian at all. But we have always agreed on hospitality. For us, hospitality is not something that happens only in the front of the house. It isn't just about the guests. You must be hospitable to your coworkers, vendors, and neighbors as well as the guests. And, of course, we are hospitable to each other.

SARAH "Hospitality is a lifestyle." I heard those words during a lecture by my mentor in a service class at the Culinary Institute of America. The person I wanted to become in the industry was crystal clear after that day. I was leaning toward back of the house at the time, but the lifestyle part sold me. The idea of being hospitable to everyone seemed so powerful. My mentor always said the first thought that crossed his mind when he woke up was, "How many days can I make today?" There is something so simple and beautiful about making a person's day with food and gracious service.

The kitchen has to be hospitable, too, especially to the front-of-the-house staff. If the kitchen is mean to the servers, the servers are mean to their customers, and then the customers go home and are mean to their children. And then the children grow up to be jerks—and difficult diners. Our menu and concept are pretty sacred to us, so we don't sacrifice the quality of a product for a guest's request. It can be difficult to say no, but sometimes we have to—in a hospitable way, of course.

EMMA As a chef, you have to trust the people who are delivering your product to the world. Sarah has never asked me to do something she knows I wouldn't want to do to my food or to eat myself. And on the rare occasion when a really challenging customer is in the restaurant, I know she always has my back. I will never forget the first time we had a difficult woman who wanted a "simply cooked piece of fish." She was so unpleasant that Sarah decided just to try to feed her and get her out of the dining room as quickly as possible. After she got her fish, the customer asked to see a manager. When Sarah went to speak with her, the woman began to complain that I should be more creative by adding some vegetables, such as asparagus, to the dish. Sarah explained that it was the middle of winter and we didn't have that vegetable. And then Sarah told her that the chef was creative and that what she had asked for was a creation of hers, not ours.

We are day makers. Magicians even. We accept
the challenge of a bad day and turn grumpiness
into giddiness. If a diner manages to leave Sorella
unhappy, he or she is somehow impervious to our
powers. Or very jaded. Or just mean. We know that
you cannot make somebody a nicer person.
And remaining gracious and hospitable takes work
in a city that can be pretty harsh. In fact, it is almost
never easy, in part because the customer is not
always right. The reward in hospitality is constant.
Spend your time making days, and, as we like
to say, everyday can be the "bestdayever."

OUR FIRST NIGHT

Thank the construction gods for a sneaky
closet and other hiding places, without which
we could not have opened the day we did.
Our first night became an ever-changing date
during the last month of building out our
space. Then it happened so fast at the end.
We decided to open with a friends-and-family
party the night before Thanksgiving in 2008.

We gave guests about forty-eight hours'
notice for the opening night party.
We decided on three passed hors d'oeuvres
to introduce our friends to what we thought
would become our signature dishes:
mini pâtés, anchovy bites, and *tonnato*
crostini—and, of course, *grissini*. Our pastry
chef Yarisis made Torta di Marsala bites
for dessert. The day leading up to the
party was insane—and the party lasted
until six o'clock the next morning.

SARAH The day of our opening, I was running around buying odds and ends until the sun went down: candleholders, business-card holders, toilet-paper stands—all of the little stuff. When I got back to Sorella, there was almost no time left before the guests would start arriving. I opened up the sneaky closet that we had built and the bench across from the bathroom that conveniently had storage space beneath it. I announced to the staff that these were the places to put any crap that was left around from construction. Both spots filled up in a snap. Cleanup was followed by a quick meeting during which we shared details about the food, and then we just went with it. I had intended to go home and change into something nicer, but time ran out, so I was in jeans and Converse sneakers. I think it was a full year before we addressed the random stuff in the sneaky closet and under that bench.

The party went fast, and before we knew it, it was five in the morning. We made an announcement that the party was over, but nobody could hear it because a bunch of people were chanting Emma's name. Within the next hour, we were able to clear out all of the revelers. We must have been drunk, but we were so excited and tired that it didn't matter. We walked home together in complete silence as the sun came up. When we got there, we still didn't talk. As we hugged goodnight and looked at each other, we both realized that it had only just begun, and that the first night had been the easy part. We were having Thanksgiving dinner in twelve hours at Sorella with our families and some industry orphans who didn't have anywhere else to go.

EMMA Those industry orphans ended up having to make the Thanksgiving dinner, too, because I didn't wake up that afternoon until after five o'clock.

SARAH Yeah, Emma, and while you were fast asleep, I was up by ten that morning and on my way to Penn Station to meet my family!

That very first night, the restaurant looked
so beautiful with people in it. Our dream
was actually happening. We knew we were
opening a restaurant, but it didn't seem real
until that evening. The next day, Sorella
still looked great, and luckily nothing was
destroyed. Someone did steal our soap
dispenser, however, which was really weird.

QUALCOSA SUL NOSTRO CIBO
(A LITTLE SOMETHING ABOUT OUR FOOD)

EMMA Food has an amazing ability to evoke emotion, and a lot of emotion goes into creating food. I've always wanted our food to be thoughtful, though never overthought. That's how I see Italian food, and that's why its simplicity and its purity of ingredients have made it my favorite cuisine.

I look to the grandmothers of Italy for inspiration. I don't believe in manipulating ingredients to make them seem like something else. When creating recipes, I think about balance and texture. I started cooking when I was four years old. I would stay up watching the Food Network and then try to create dishes. Because I was so young, sometimes what I made was gross, but I made my parents try it anyway. They took me out with them to the best restaurants, and, as I got older, I would try to re-create what I had tasted. I have not worked in many restaurants, but I have eaten in a shitload of them.

SARAH ON EMMA From the moment I met Emma, she became my favorite person to eat with. We have overordered and overeaten at more restaurants than I can even begin to name. The first time she cooked for me, I was blown away. After that, she would re-create something we had eaten at a restaurant, and it would be spot on. When we started conceptualizing the menu for Sorella and she started making her own food, I would laugh out loud at how shockingly good it was. The flavors of her food make it seem more complicated than it is, but I think that's because she balances things so well. She cooks with integrity and honesty and makes food that is incredibly tasty.

ECONOMIZZA
ACQUA, BEVI VINO
(CONSERVE WATER, DRINK WINE)

SARAH You know how they say you have to immerse yourself in another culture to really learn a language? It's the same with wine: it involves a whole lot of drinking—or, rather, tasting. I never wanted textbook-style knowledge. I wanted to be able to describe the way wine tasted, in my own words, from my own experience. I am an immersion learner.

I learned how to write a wine list by writing a wine list. Just like I learned how to run a restaurant by running one. When I went through the wine program in culinary school, I was only twenty years old. I didn't get it, to say the least. I thought it all tasted the same, like alcohol. I would talk to my instructor after class in hopes of gaining some brilliant insight that would open my palate to the experiences my classmates were describing. But he always said it just would click. My fellow culinarians would yell out flavors they were tasting and smells they were smelling, which made me feel both challenged and crazy. Hints of lychee and fresh-cut grass, rich dark fruits and tobacco, even cat pee and manure. I felt defeated daily. The first time it clicked for me was with a sparkling Moscato d'Asti from Vietti. It could have been the low alcohol that allowed me to taste and smell all the fruit. Whatever it was, it happened. The fragrance of ripe peaches slapped me in the face. The fruit followed through on the palate, too. When I became accustomed to the taste of alcohol, I was able to get down with wine tasting.

I focused on what I could understand and articulate well, namely the palate. If I wanted to know how wine was made, how the soil impacts the taste, and all that other stuff that fancy wine folks talk about, I knew that I would have to make wine. That's just the kind of learner I am. So for now I have stuck with what I do best. On the rare occasion that I get a specific question about altitude, soil, or the like, I am thankful for my smartphone and Google.

I got into Italian wine during my fellowship at Caterina restaurant at the culinary institute. It had an all-Italian wine list, and because it was a student-run,

classroom kind of place, we were always learning about Italian wine. Most people are intimidated by Italian wines because of the labels. It takes a certain level of understanding to be able to decipher the information. For example, the grape doesn't always appear, which freaks people out. It's been my mission since opening Sorella to make our diners comfortable with what they are drinking.

Our wine program is thoughtful and just right for our food and vibe. The wines tend to be on the younger side, because we don't have storage space for aging wines or for old bottles. I also like to keep the vintages young because we are a young vintage. I look for offbeat varietals and youthful producers to keep the list fresh, and I buy wines that I enjoy drinking myself. Italian wines have a balance that appeals to me, and they are particularly food friendly. Many people are the most familiar with only the expensive ones, like Barolo and Brunello. But I like to sell a Nebbiolo that's affordable and explain how it's the same grape as Barolo, which is also a place. I love watching it click for the staff, too. I tend to talk a server through a wine sale rather than go in for the sell myself. I don't want the servers to hide behind me. I want them to be confident about everything that we offer. I am still learning, and when I learn something cool and new about a wine, I like to pass that information along to my staff and customers. The day I am done learning about the wines we sell, I hope to move to Italy and make wine. Then I can talk about all the fancy stuff.

EMMA ON SARAH I always let Sarah pick the wine when we go out to eat. I also text her questions when I am dining without her. She is like my human version of *Wine for Dummies*. I love the fact that she doesn't overthink the wine too much. Basically, her choice comes down to one determining factor: does it taste good? This is very much my mentality with food, too. I dislike overthought food. It never comes out as good or as natural. That compatibility in approach is one of the many reasons why Sarah's wines work so well with my food. Sarah could hold a wine tasting with a group of eight-year-olds, and I bet a million dollars they would walk away with simple yet insightful wine knowledge that most thirty-five-year-olds don't have. She breaks down the walls of intimidation of the wine puzzle and makes it tasty and fun.

HOW WE
KEEP IT TOGETHER

To say that restaurant professionals and industry folks abuse their bodies is an understatement. The hours are crazy, we spend lots of time standing, and there is quite a bit of physical labor. Oh, yeah, and the vices: the cigarettes, the drinking, the eating, the drinking. Our friendship had been built on those vices. Creating Sorella was rough on our bodies with menu tastings, wine tastings, eating and drinking research, long hours, and inhaling construction dust and the not-so-fresh Chinatown air.

EMMA I started doing Pilates whenever I had the chance. Sarah called it "plotskies" and made fun of me every time I went. I became obsessed. I had been a dancer in high school and enjoyed the movement, and it started to change my body.

SARAH The Sorella opening was superintense, both physically and emotionally. Those were the most trying moments of our relationship, in a good way. We had only each other, and we were terrified. We were so young—even younger than we thought. We were open six days a week, from six o'clock at night to two in the morning. And we had to run a business. Getting out of bed those first few months was the hardest thing imaginable. Emma had talked to me a bunch about Pilates, and one night hunched over the computer in the world's smallest and hottest office, I signed up for some sessions. I should mention that I was topless, because it was the only way I could do bookkeeping in the office without fainting from the radiant heat of the boiler. Pilates became more appealing when I could no longer ignore the state of my midsection. Emma recommended her instructor, Ashley Deleon, and there was a three-week wait for an opening. Ashley changed my life, and I started to go whenever I could.

EMMA We would sneak out midday or go on our days off. Sarah waited for a while to take classes because she was self-conscious.

SARAH Pilates opened the door to other forms of exercise. I started running the Williamsburg bridge during family meal, and Emma got really into yoga.

We have continued working with Ashley. She has known our bodies from the opening and now through the running of Sorella. She has helped with crooked hips from bussing tables and tight cooking spaces and has turned hunched shoulders into proud chests. We have passed knowledge of proper stretching and standing to our staff and will forever be advocates of a healthy spine.

KITCHEN'S CHOICE

At Sorella, the kitchen chooses the music. Here are some of our favorite songs to cook to while our guests eat to the same tunes.

last caress • **THE MISFITS**

soul kitchen • **THE DOORS**

is this love • **BOB MARLEY & THE WAILERS**

end of the line • **THE TRAVELING WILBURYS**

i wanna be your dog • **THE STOOGES**

rocky raccoon • **THE BEATLES**

gut feeling • **DEVO**

everybody knows this is nowhere • **NEIL YOUNG**

excitable boy • **WARREN ZEVON**

tiny dancer • **ELTON JOHN**

blitzkrieg bop • **RAMONES**

wu tang clan ain't nuthin ta f' wit • **WU-TANG CLAN**

can't you hear me knocking • **THE ROLLING STONES**

sweet thing • **VAN MORRISON**

because the night • **PATTI SMITH**

hey • **PIXIES**

once in a lifetime • **TALKING HEADS**

baby baby • **THE VIBRATORS**

sinister kid • **THE BLACK KEYS**

there is a light that never goes out • **THE SMITHS**

tom sawyer • **RUSH**

the w.a.n.d. • **THE FLAMING LIPS**

make it wit chu • **QUEENS OF THE STONE AGE**

she's a mystery to me • **ROY ORBISON**

wild night • **VAN MORRISON**

reuben and cherise • **JERRY GARCIA BAND**

livin' thing • **ELECTRIC LIGHT ORCHESTRA**

20th century boy • **T. REX**

camellia • **HALL & OATES**

apple scruffs • **GEORGE HARRISON**

cowboy song • **THIN LIZZY**

that's all you need • **FACES**

the rain song • **LED ZEPPELIN**

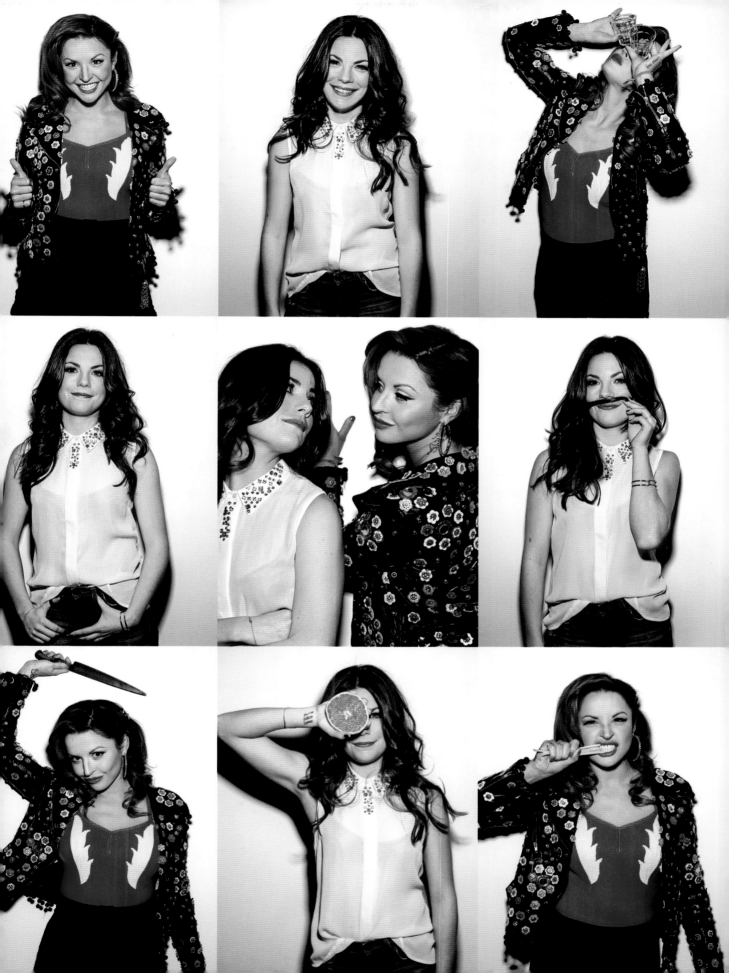

COCKTAILS

We opened Sorella with only a beer and wine license. That was all we could get at the time because our community board wasn't accepting applications for new liquor licenses. The reason? It just wasn't.

The truth is, the process of acquiring and keeping a liquor license is quite weird and often sketchy. In our second year, we were somehow able to get one. Emma was all about serving cocktails but I wasn't really excited to do them. I had never been a bartender, and cocktails always gave me a horrible hangover. I made rules for how I would approach the beverage program, and originated drinks with the same mindset that we bring to creating recipes for food. These cocktails are based on interesting small-batch liquors, flavors I like, balance, and simplicity. I choose one brand for each spirit and that is our house pour. Through lots and lots of research, I have found that poor-quality liquor in cocktails is what causes hangovers, not the cocktails themselves.

Over the years, the drink menu at Sorella has evolved, thanks to collaborations with the talented individuals with whom I work, who force me to try new things. I always name the drinks, though; it's my favorite part of the process.

OCA ZAMPEROSEE

SERVES 1

The name of this drink is Italian for "pink-footed goose," which has no real relevance except the drink is pink from the Campari. My sense of humor often sneaks onto the menu, and I thought the bizarre name would get customers to ask me what it meant and then be tickled by its randomness. But as it turns out, it's one of those names that makes them point at the menu and say, "I don't know how to pronounce it but I'll have this."

Salt for rimming the glass

1 lime wedge (optional), plus ½ fl oz (15 ml) fresh lime juice

1½ fl oz (45 ml) Blat vodka

¾ fl oz (25 ml) Campari

1½ fl oz (45 ml) fresh grapefruit juice

Splash of fresh orange juice

¼ fl oz (8 ml) Simple Syrup (page 40)

Grapefruit twist for garnish

Pour salt onto a small plate. Moisten the rim of a rocks glass with the lime wedge or water. Invert the glass and dip the rim in the salt to coat.

Fill a shaker glass with ice. Layer in the vodka, Campari, citrus juices, and simple syrup. Cover and shake vigorously. Carefully fill the salt-rimmed glass with fresh ice and strain in the contents of the shaker glass. Garnish with the grapefruit twist and serve.

GINSALATA

SERVES 1

When I worked in the kitchen at the Pegu Club in Soho, I became obsessed with the combination of gin and cucumber. Green juices had become popular, and people were into drinking salads. *Insalata* means "salad," ergo the Ginsalata.

2 fl oz (60 ml) Death's Door gin
2 fl oz (60 ml) cucumber juice (see note)
1 fl oz (30 ml) fresh lime juice
¾ fl oz (25 ml) Basil Syrup (page 40)
Pickle slice for garnish

Fill a shaker glass with ice. Layer in the gin, cucumber juice, lime juice, and syrup. Cover and shake vigorously. Strain into a highball glass filled with fresh ice. Garnish with the pickle and serve.

Note: To make the cucumber juice, peel 1 cucumber and purée in a blender or juicer. Refrigerate the extra juice in an airtight container for up to 1 week.

THE HONEYPOT

SERVES 1

This was my very first cocktail creation. It doesn't have honey in it, which sometimes causes confusion, so I share the embarrassing fact that it is named after Winnie the Pooh's honeypot, which is what I think it looks like. The caramel-rimmed glass was pretty much a stroke of genius.

½ cup (4 oz/125 g) sugar

1 cup (8 oz/250 ml) heavy cream

½ tsp vanilla extract

Tiny pinch of salt

2 fl oz (60 ml) Old Overholt rye whiskey

¾ fl oz (25 ml) fresh lemon juice

½ fl oz (15 ml) Caramel Syrup (page 40)

2 dashes of bitters

Lemon twist for garnish

To make the caramel, warm the sugar in a saucepan over medium heat until amber. Lower the heat and slowly add the cream, stirring constantly. Bring to a boil and stir to dissolve the sugar. Add the vanilla and salt, strain, and let cool completely.

Pour a little caramel into a shallow dish. Invert a rocks glass and dip the rim into the caramel to coat. (Refrigerate the remaining caramel in an airtight container for up to 2 weeks).

Fill a shaker glass with ice. Layer in the rye, lemon juice, syrup, and bitters. Cover and shake vigorously. Carefully fill the caramel-rimmed glass with fresh ice and strain in the contents of the shaker glass. Garnish with the lemon twist and serve.

a good
MARGARITA

SERVES 1

The margarita is my favorite.
I used to say it was my favorite
summer cocktail, but I have
discovered that you can drink
it year-round. Emma turned
me on to the margarita, and
while we were roommates,
I perfected a recipe that we both
regard as the best one ever.
To be humble, however, we
refer to it as a good one.

Salt for rimming the glass
2 fl oz (60 ml) Excellia tequila blanco
1 fl oz (30 ml) fresh lime juice
¾ fl oz (25 ml) fresh lemon juice
¼ fl oz (8 ml) fresh orange juice
¾ fl oz (25 ml) Simple Syrup
(page 40) or honey
Lime wedge for garnish

Pour salt onto a small plate. Moisten
the rim of a rocks glass with a lime
wedge or water. Invert the glass
and dip the rim in the salt to coat.

Fill a shaker glass with ice. Layer
in the tequila, citrus juices, and
syrup. Cover and shake vigorously.
Strain into a rocks glass filled
with fresh ice. Garnish with
the lime wedge and serve.

THE CUBAN MEX

SERVES 1

I don't enjoy spicy cocktails, but the rest of the world seems to. This is a creation by Jonathan Deleon, who is a dear member of the Sorella permanent family and broke our hearts when he moved away.

Salt for rimming the glass

1 lime wedge (optional), plus
1 fl oz (30 ml) fresh lime juice

2 fl oz (60 ml) Excellia tequila blanco

1 fl oz (30 ml) store-bought guava purée or juice

¾ fl oz (25 ml) fresh lemon juice

¾ fl oz Habanero Syrup (page 40)

Lime wheel for garnish

Pour salt onto a small plate. Moisten half of the rim of a rocks glass with the lime wedge or water. Invert the glass and dip the moistened half of the rim in the salt to coat (this gives the drinker a choice of flavors, the best of both worlds).

Fill a shaker glass with ice. Layer in the tequila, guava purée, citrus juices, and syrup. Cover and shake vigorously. Carefully fill the salt-rimmed glass with fresh ice and strain in the contents of the shaker glass. Garnish with the lime wheel and serve.

THE CHERRY GODMOTHER

SERVES 1

This is an updated version of the classic cocktail The Godfather. The name makes me smile every time.

2½ fl oz (75 ml) Wemyss blended malt Scotch whisky

¼ fl oz (8 ml) amaretto

¼ fl oz (8 ml) Luxardo maraschino liqueur

Dash of bitters

Stemmed cherry or orange twist for garnish

Fill a shaker glass with ice. Layer in the Scotch, amaretto, maraschino liqueur, and bitters. Stir vigorously. Strain into a martini glass and serve up, garnished with the cherry.

HERBS ON VACATION
SERVES 1

My bartender and dear friend Logan invented this cocktail with me. We have a lot of fun chatting about drinks, and he is always asking me to carry a new spirit. Although I love Fernet-Branca, I had not added it to our shelves because I was stubborn and felt that we just didn't need another digestivo! Logan eventually wore me down, and we discussed the idea of combining it with rum. The minty, herbaceous quality has always been what I love about Fernet, and rum makes me think of being on vacation.

Fresh mint leaf for garnish

1½ fl oz (45 ml) Blackwell rum

½ fl oz (15 ml) Fernet-Branca

1 fl oz (30 ml) fresh lime juice

½ fl oz (15 ml) honey

Dash of pineapple bitters

Slap the mint leaf. (Literally, slap that leaf! You don't want to crush, tear, or bruise it, but you do want to bring out the essential oils and aroma.) Fill a shaker glass with ice. Layer in the rum, Fernet-Branca, lime juice, honey, and bitters. Stir vigorously. Strain into a martini glass and serve up, garnished with the mint leaf.

SIMPLE SYRUP

MAKES 375 ML (12 FL OZ)

1 cup (8 fl oz/250 ml) water   1 cup (8 oz/250 g) sugar

In a saucepan over medium-high heat, bring the water to a simmer. Add the sugar and stir until completely dissolved. Remove from the heat and let cool to room temperature. Pour the syrup into a jar or bottle, cap, and refrigerate until needed.

CARAMEL SYRUP

MAKES 375 ML (12 FL OZ)

1 cup (8 oz/250 g) sugar   Pinch of salt

1 cup (8 fl oz/250 ml) water

In a heavy saucepan over medium-high heat, warm the sugar until it turns an amber color. Lower the heat and slowly add the water. Raise the heat to medium-high and bring to a boil, stirring until the sugar has dissolved. Add the salt. Remove from the heat and let cool to room temperature. Pour the syrup into a jar or bottle, cap, and refrigerate until needed.

BASIL SYRUP

MAKES 375 ML (12 FL OZ)

1 cup (8 fl oz/250 ml) water   Leaves from 1 bunch
                                    fresh basil
1 cup (8 oz/250 g) sugar

In a saucepan over medium-high heat, bring the water to a simmer. Add the sugar and stir until completely dissolved. Remove from the heat, add the basil, and let cool to room temperature. Pour the syrup, including the basil, into a jar or bottle, cap, and refrigerate until needed.

HABANERO SYRUP

MAKES 375 ML (12 FL OZ)

1 cup (8 fl oz/250 ml) water   ½ cup (2 oz/60 g) chopped
                                    habanero chiles
1 cup (8 oz/250 g) sugar

In a saucepan over medium-high heat, bring the water to a simmer. Add the sugar and stir until completely dissolved. Remove from the heat, add the chiles, and let cool to room temperature. Pour the syrup, including the chiles, into a jar or bottle, cap, and refrigerate until needed.

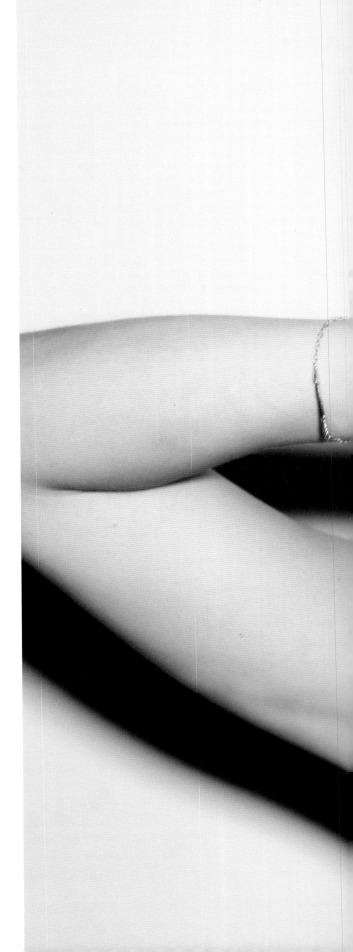

GRISSINI
AT SORELLA

In Piedmont, *grissini* were one of the constants we made sure to consume daily (along with *agnolotti dal plin* and *tajarin al burro*). We connected with a great guide, Sandro, during our stay. His fee was meals and the cost of gas, and he took us to restaurants that we wouldn't have been able to get into or probably even find. Sandro was a Turin native and had a very special and critical love for the local *grissini*. He took us where his favorite version was served, but like most Italian men, he spoke of his mother's *grissini* with the greatest fondness. He introduced us to many versions of this salty, addictive table snack, which were ubiquitous in restaurants. Indeed, they literally kept arriving all the way through the meal, and Sandro even ate them during dessert.

The *grissini* came in different thicknesses and lengths. Some were light and airy, almost soft. Others were dense and crazy crunchy. We ate them at meals, during the *aperitivo* hour, and as late-night snacks in our hotel room. (We learned of the *grissini* with *tonnato* sauce combo through room service at our hotel in Alba.) Our trip was for inspiration, and these classic Piemontese breadsticks were certainly inspiring. We decided that we had to serve the best in the city at Sorella. Our pastry chef, Yarisis, researched, tested, tasted, and tasted again to perfect the *grissini* we serve. We are not sharing the recipe, only a peekaboo at the process. To experience them, you have to visit. Maybe we'll include the recipe in our next book.

Grissini are part of the Sorella experience, at the bar and in the dining room, whether you're sipping a cocktail or having a bite.

QUALCOSINA

Carne Cruda 48

Marinated Mussels with Stracciatella 51

Baccalà Mantecato with Cantaloupe, Chiles, and Homemade Potato Chips 54

Pork Rillette 57

Acciughe al Verde 58

Grilled Summer Squash with Ricotta, Balsamic, and Ciabatta 61

Pâté di Fegato 64

Spinach and Kale Dip with Orange-Walnut Gremolata 67

Heirloom Tomato Salad with Bagna Cauda 68

Escarole Salad with Hazelnuts and Pecorino 71

Kale Salad and Squashes, Almonds, and Grana 72

Broccoli Fritto 75

Radish and Fennel Salad with Goat's Milk Butter, Torn Herbs, and Orange Gastrique 76

Shaved Brussels Sprouts Salad with Charred Red Onion 79

Beet Salad with Honeyed Ricotta, Pistachios, and Kale Chips 82

Fava and Pea Salad 84

Arugula and Prosciutto Salad with Pickled Pears and Roasted Pear Vinaigrette 85

Grilled Corn Salad with Chile-Lime Dressing and Corn Bread Croutons 87

Watermelon and Cucumber Salad with Goat Cheese and Sweet Shallots 88

Spring Lamb Tongue with Black Lentil, Caramelized Shallot, and Artichoke Confit 90

Crispy Veal Sweetbreads with Dipping Sauces 91

Warm Sherried Mushroom Salad with Hijiki and Pine Nut Purée 93

Stuffed Onion with Fonduta, Amaretti, and Sage 94

When you love to eat as much as we do, it's more fun to eat lots of different bites than lots of bites of the same thing. *Qualcosina* means "a little something," and it is what we call our small plates at Sorella. We describe them as elevated appetizers, with some more filling than others. Every Saturday night, without fail, some guest says, "Oh, these are like tapas!" And we have to say, "No guys, these are not tapas. Tapas are from Spain." These tasty dishes can act as starters, if that's what you are looking for. But they will also make a wonderful family-style feast if you feel like making several of them and calling them dinner. Some work well as passed hors d'oeuvres for a party and others as a savory snack at midafternoon or midnight. Most important, they convey a sense of the balance that we consistently strive for between innovation and tradition.

CARNE CRUDA

SERVES 4

In Piedmont, this dish is always made with veal and, during fall, is smothered with truffle shavings. That is how we first tasted it. Since serving raw veal is not as common here, our version features grass-fed beef from the humanely raised cattle of Hearst Ranch.

1½ lb (750 g) high-quality beef such as top round, trimmed of excess fat and cut into small dice

⅓ cup (3 fl oz/90 ml) extra-virgin olive oil

Kosher salt

FOR *the* SALAD

5 oz (155 g) sugar snap peas, trimmed and julienned

1½ oz (45 g) Podda Classico or Parmesan cheese, broken into tiny crumbles

3 Tbsp fresh lemon juice

Extra-virgin olive oil for drizzling

Salt and freshly ground pepper

FOR *the* CRISPY SHALLOTS

4 shallots

½ cup (4 fl oz/125 ml) whole milk

Vegetable oil for deep-frying

1 cup (5 oz/155 g) all-purpose flour

Kosher salt

Lemon Aioli (page 230) for serving

Put the beef in a bowl and add the olive oil and a hefty pinch of salt. Massage the seasoned oil into the meat with your hands for about 2 minutes. Set aside.

To make the salad, in a bowl, toss together the peas and cheese. Sprinkle in the lemon juice, drizzle with olive oil, and season with salt to taste and a grind or two of pepper. Toss again to mix well. Set aside.

To make the crispy shallots, using a mandoline or a sharp chef's knife, cut the shallots into paper-thin slices. Put the shallots in a bowl, add the milk, and soak for about 10 minutes. Meanwhile, pour oil into a small saucepan to a depth of 2 inches (5 cm) and heat over high heat to 360°F (185°C). Sift together the flour and 1 tsp salt onto a plate. Drain the shallots and dredge them in the seasoned flour. Shake off any excess flour. Add to the hot oil and fry until golden, about 10 minutes. Using a slotted spoon or skimmer, transfer to a paper towel to drain. Season with salt.

to ASSEMBLE Divide the beef into 4 equal portions. Place a ring mold on each serving plate and fill with the beef. Make a swoosh of aioli on the plate. Place a mound of the salad on each plate, matching the size of the ring mold. Top the beef with the warm shallots. Remove the ring molds and serve right away.

MARINATED MUSSELS

with

STRACCIATELLA

SERVES 6–8

In many parts of Italy, combining seafood and cheese is considered a major offense. Fortunately, we decided to overlook this small cultural law when this dish made its debut on *Iron Chef*. The marinade is best if prepared a day or two in advance. It also makes a terrific dressing for vegetables, such as blanched or steamed English peas, asparagus, or fennel.

FOR *the* MARINADE

1 cup (1 oz/30 g) fresh basil leaves, roughly chopped

1 cup (1 oz/30 g) fresh mint leaves, roughly chopped

1 cup (1 oz/30 g) fresh flat-leaf parsley leaves, roughly chopped

½ large head garlic, finely chopped

1 Tbsp kosher salt

1 Tbsp red pepper flakes

2 cups (16 fl oz/500 ml) extra-virgin olive oil

Grated zest and juice of 1 large orange

Grated zest and juice of 2 large lemons

Freshly ground black pepper

4–6 lb (2–3 kg) mussels, scrubbed and debearded

About 1 bottle (24 fl oz/750 ml) dry white wine

5 shallots, chopped

1–2 lemons, quartered

1–2 oranges, quartered

A few bay leaves

About 3 cups (24 fl oz/750 ml) Homemade Stracciatella (page 63) for serving

1 loaf good-quality ciabatta, thickly sliced

Extra-virgin olive oil for brushing

Torn fresh basil leaves for garnish

Freshly ground black pepper

To make the marinade, in a bowl, combine the herbs, garlic, salt, red pepper flakes, olive oil, orange zest and juice, lemon zest and juice, and a generous amount of black pepper and stir to mix well. Cover and refrigerate overnight or for up to 2 days.

Discard any open mussels or mussels that do not close to the touch. Make sure you sniff them as well; they should smell fresh and briny. Discard any that smell fishy or "off."

In a large rondeau or other wide, shallow pot over medium-high heat, combine the mussels, wine, and about 1 cup (8 fl oz/250 ml) water. Add the shallots, lemons, oranges, and bay leaves, adjusting the amount depending on how many mussels are in your pot and how big your fruits are. Cover and steam, shaking the covered pot once in a while, until the mussels open, 3–5 minutes. Drain and discard the liquid. Discard any mussels that failed to open. Take the mussels out of their shells and place them in the marinade. Let stand for about 20 minutes at room temperature or up to overnight in the refrigerator.

Meanwhile, make the stracciatella as directed.

to ASSEMBLE When the mussels are very flavorful from the marinade and you are ready to serve, grill or toast the ciabatta. For each diner, brush 1 or 2 slices of ciabatta with olive oil and grill or broil until nicely browned and toasty, about 1 minute per side. Arrange the toasts on a platter. Top each piece of toast with a heaping spoonful of the stracciatella, followed by a spoonful of the mussels and a drizzle of the marinade. Garnish with basil and a grind of black pepper and serve right away.

IRON CHEF

We got a call from the Food Network asking Emma to audition for *The Next Iron Chef* reality competition series. Emma never wanted to do any type of reality TV and was firm about that, but she went for the screen test anyway. She pretty much told them that she would not do that particular show but that she would love to do an *Iron Chef* battle.

SARAH I always wanted Emma to do television. She is great on camera, so natural and confident, with no filter.

EMMA Yeah, I had definitely said some things that I thought were going to cause a wee bit of trouble. I was so excited when I got the call to do an *Iron Chef* battle. When I was little, I'd stay up all night watching battles on mute. The show caused me to miss a lot of school. I really wanted to battle Mario Batali, but he was no longer on the show by the time I got there. So I was up against Michael Symon, who is awesome. I was allowed to bring two sous chefs, so I brought John, my sous at the time, and Molly, my OG sous.

Mock battles started in the restaurant about a month before the actual battle. They were intense. At this point, we were told of three potential secret ingredients and developed menus for each: salt cod, passion fruit, and fresh mozzarella. The only time in the history of Sorella when there was no music playing in the kitchen was during the practice battles.

EMMA We liked the menus we came up with, but some were definitely more challenging than others—at least during practice they were. Our secret ingredient ended up being fresh mozzarella. The night before the battle, we went to dinner at Gramercy Tavern and were a little overserved, if you know what I mean. We had a sleepover at my apartment like a bunch of excited teenagers. We went to the studio together the next morning, both nervous and excited as hell. Before the battle started, we got to meet everyone, including the Chairman, a sweet and quiet man. Once the cameras started rolling, he became very intense.

SARAH Watching the battle from the audience was one of the proudest moments of my life. I had watched the practice battles, but the way Emma and her team were on the actual day was a sight to behold. Audience members were not allowed a bathroom break for a while, and I had downed a few shots of tequila to ease my nerves before the battle started. Bad idea!

EMMA We didn't get to down any shots until after the battle. We requested Jameson on all of our ingredients lists for shot purposes exclusively. We gave shots to Michael Symon's team, too. The only vessels John could find for the shots were small glass mixing bowls.

SARAH When the battle ended, it was announced that our team had one of the fastest battle times in history. It didn't have any influence on the final decision, but was pretty cool nonetheless, especially since Emma was the youngest challenger ever.

EMMA Michael Symon won, but it was still the most fun I had ever had cooking. I could do it every day. We celebrated that night in Brooklyn, and when the show aired, we threw a kick-ass viewing party at a Ping-Pong bar. Watching our battle and playing Ping-Pong together? Priceless. Although come to think of it, I never got to play that night.

SARAH The viewing party was one of my drunker evenings. I gave a speech that was unfortunately recorded, but I managed to destroy the evidence. Watching Emma cook on national television was thrilling. She was as great as I expected, and she made some really good ball jokes during meatball time. Our sous chef John drank too much and got kicked out of the party, and that made my speech seem okay.

IRON CHEF MENU

Salad of Mozzarella with
Sugar Snaps and Squash Blossoms

Marinated Mussels with
Burrata and Grilled Ciabatta

Gnocchi with Smoked Mozzarella
Fonduta, Crispy Speck, and
Scallions

Mozzarella-Stuffed Meatball
with Caramelized Onions and
Tonnato Sauce

Marinated Peaches with
Vanilla Stracciatella and
Shortbread Biscuit

BACCALÀ MANTECATO

—— *with* ——

CANTALOUPE, CHILES, *and* HOMEMADE POTATO CHIPS

SERVES 6–8

Salt cod + potato = good. So we figured, why not try it with potato chips? We like using Calabrian chiles because they are fruity and smoky and just spicy enough to maintain a nicely balanced flavor. Look for jars of whole red chiles packed in olive oil in specialty-food stores or online.

FOR *the* BACCALÀ

1 lb (500 g) salt cod fillet

2½ cups (20 fl oz/625 ml) whole milk

1 large russet potato

3 large cloves garlic, minced

⅓ cup (3 fl oz/80 ml) extra-virgin olive oil

1 Tbsp fresh lemon juice

Pinch of grated orange zest

Pinch of grated lemon zest

½ cup (4 fl oz/125 ml) heavy cream

Sea salt and freshly ground pepper (optional)

Snipped fresh chives for garnish (optional)

FOR *the* CANTALOUPE

1 small, ripe cantaloupe

2 Tbsp finely chopped Calabrian chiles

Drizzle of extra-virgin olive oil

½ lemon

FOR *the* POTATO CHIPS

Vegetable oil for deep-frying

2 large russet potatoes

Sea salt

To make the baccalà, put the salt cod in a bowl and add cold water to cover by 2 inches (5 cm). Let soak overnight in the refrigerator, changing the water a few times.

When the cod has released most of its salt and becomes pliable, drain thoroughly. It should taste perfectly seasoned and not as salty as the sea. Break it up into smaller pieces (about 4 inches/10 cm long), discarding any errant bones, and put in a saucepan. Add the milk and bring to a boil over high heat, then reduce the heat to medium-low and poach until the fish begins to flake apart, 20–25 minutes. Remove from the heat. Using a slotted spoon, transfer the cod to a bowl. Reserve the milk.

While the cod is poaching, put the potato in a small saucepan with water to cover, bring to a boil over medium-high heat, and cook until tender when pierced with a knife, 20–30 minutes. Transfer to a plate and let cool briefly, then peel and cut into chunks. Set aside.

Preheat the oven to 350°F (180°C).

Put the cod in a stand mixer fitted with the paddle attachment and beat on low speed just to break up the fish. Add the garlic, increase the speed to medium, and beat briefly to mix. On medium speed, slowly add the olive oil, lemon juice, and citrus zests and beat until well blended. Add the potato, a few chunks at a time, and whip until incorporated. On low speed, slowly add the cream. The mixture should begin to take on the texture of fluffy mashed potatoes. If it is too thick, add some of the poaching milk to thin it out a bit. Add some pepper, if you like, then taste the mixture to see if it needs a pinch of salt. If the cod soaked for a bit too long, you may need to add some. Scrape the baccalà into several small ramekins or an ovenproof serving dish and warm gently in the oven while you season the cantaloupe and make the potato chips.

To make the cantaloupe, halve the melon, scoop out and discard the seeds, and cut away the rind. Cut the flesh into very small pieces, about the size of a pinkie nail or the dice for salsa. In a bowl, combine the cantaloupe, chiles, and olive oil. Add a squeeze of lemon juice and toss to mix and coat. Set aside.

To make the potato chips, pour oil into a saucepan or deep fryer to a depth of 3 inches (7.5 cm) and heat over high heat to 360°F (185°C). Meanwhile, using a mandoline or a sharp chef's knife, cut the potatoes lengthwise into paper-thin slices. Toss a handful of the potato slices into the hot oil, being careful not to crowd the pan, and fry until golden. Using a skimmer or slotted spoon, transfer to paper towels to drain. Sprinkle the chips with salt while they are still warm. Repeat to cook the remaining chips.

to ASSEMBLE Remove the warm baccalà from the oven. Top with the cantaloupe mixture and garnish with some chives, if you like. Serve warm with the chips for dipping.

PORK RILLETTE

We refer to the pork rillette portion of the meal as "pork butter & jelly time" because this dish is essentially an awesome riff on a PB&J sandwich. Nothing complements this fatty, luscious spread better than strawberry jam. For more great accompaniment choices, see pages 231–232.

About 2 cups (1 lb/500 g) rendered bacon fat (from about 3 lb/1.5 kg bacon)

2 lb (1 kg) boneless pork butt, cut into 2-inch (5-cm) pieces

½ yellow onion, finely chopped

4 cloves garlic, chopped

½ cup (4 fl oz/125 ml) dry white wine

2 bay leaves

Kosher salt

Grated zest and juice of 1 lemon

Buttermilk Country Bread (page 227) for serving

Strawberry Jam (page 231) for serving

Chopped fresh basil for serving

Preheat the oven to 225°F (110°C).

In a large Dutch oven or other heavy ovenproof pot over medium heat, melt the bacon fat completely. Add the pork butt, onion, garlic, wine, bay leaves, and a big pinch of salt and stir to mix well. Cover and place in the oven. Cook slowly until the meat is super tender and falls apart with the touch of a fork, about 3½ hours.

Remove from the oven and let cool slightly. Pour off the fat from the meat and reserve. Discard the bay leaves and place the pork and onion mixture in a food processor. Drizzle in about ½ cup (4 fl oz/125 ml) of the reserved fat and pulse the mixture until a chunky paste forms.

Now comes the time to season—heavily. Do not fear salt here. The flavor you're trying to achieve is salty, porky, fatty goodness. While you're stirring and seasoning, go ahead and add the lemon zest and juice; they will brighten things up a bit and give some pop. Scrape into a serving bowl or a few small ramekins and serve right away with the bread, jam, and basil.

SARAH'S *drink note* Sip Champagne. The bubbles are a refreshing counterpoint to the unctuous pork spread, and the toastiness of good Champagne will complement the jam's cooked sugar flavor and the yeasty country bread.

ACCIUGHE AL VERDE

Here's our luxurious take on a traditional Piemontese dish. At Sorella, we serve it deconstructed, but when you put everything together, it becomes what we call "the best bite." Use salt-packed anchovies, which are clean tasting and firm.

FOR *the* LEMON BUTTER

½ cup (4 oz/125 g) unsalted butter, at room temperature

Grated zest of 4 lemons

1 tsp kosher salt

FOR *the* SALSA VERDE

½ cup (¾ oz/20 g) roughly chopped fresh basil

½ cup (¾ oz/20 g) roughly chopped fresh flat-leaf parsley

3 cloves garlic, minced

½ Tbsp red pepper flakes

1 tsp kosher salt

1 cup (8 fl oz/250 ml) extra-virgin olive oil

½ cup (2½ oz/75 g) hazelnuts

1 can (4 oz/125 g) salt-packed anchovies, preferably Ligurian

Extra-virgin olive oil as needed

Flatbread for serving, homemade (page 223) or good-quality store-bought

3 hard-boiled egg yolks, passed through a sieve

To make the lemon butter, put the butter in a bowl. Using a wooden spoon or an electric mixer, beat until light and fluffy. Add the lemon zest and throw in the salt. Beat until incorporated. Cover and refrigerate for at least 24 hours or up to 2 weeks. Bring to room temperature before serving.

To make the salsa verde, in a bowl, stir together the basil, parsley, garlic, red pepper flakes, and salt. Slowly pour in the olive oil while stirring constantly. When the salsa is thoroughly mixed, taste and adjust the seasoning. When you're satisfied with the flavor, cover and refrigerate for at least 24 hours or up to 1 week.

When you're ready to serve, preheat the oven to 350°F (180°C). Spread the hazelnuts on a baking sheet and toast in the oven until the color darkens a little and the skins start to blister, 10–15 minutes. Pour the hot nuts onto a clean kitchen towel, gather up the corners of the towel, let steam for 1 minute, then rub vigorously in the towel to remove the skins. Chop roughly and set aside.

Gently rinse the anchovies under cold running water to remove the salt and any impurities. Working with 1 anchovy at a time, and using a paring knife, carefully split the anchovy open along the belly, dividing it into 2 fillets. Using the tip of the knife, lift out and discard the spine. Remove the tail, fins, head, and any excess muck, rinse briefly again, and pat dry. Fillet the remaining anchovies the same way. If you will not be assembling the anchovy bites right away, line a small plastic container with parchment paper and lay the fillets on the parchment as they are ready. Pour in olive oil just to cover and cover the container. Refrigerate until needed.

to ASSEMBLE Smear about 1 tsp room-temperature lemon butter on a piece of flatbread and top with an anchovy fillet. Using a fork, scoop up ½ tsp salsa verde, letting the excess oil drip off, and place it on the anchovy. Then sprinkle on some hazelnuts and egg yolk. Repeat to assemble more anchovy bites, making about 4 bites per person. Serve as a passed hors d'oeuvre or on a family-style platter. Store the leftover salsa and lemon butter for other uses.

SARAH'S *drink note* This dish may be a little scary to some because of the unwarranted negativity that often surrounds anchovies. Loosen up with a nice vodka and soda with lime. We like Blat, a Spanish vodka made in the Canary Islands that has a clean taste and no impurities. Wash down this favorite bite with a sparkling wine, preferably a Grower Champagne.

GRILLED
SUMMER SQUASH

—— *with* ——

RICOTTA, BALSAMIC, *and* CIABATTA

——◆ SERVES 6–8 ◆——

3 lb (1.5 kg) assorted summer squashes, any combination, trimmed and cut into slices ½–1 inch (12 mm–2.5 cm) thick

Kosher salt and freshly ground black pepper

Extra-virgin olive oil for drizzling and brushing

1 plump head garlic, chopped

1½ cups (1½ oz/45 g) packed fresh basil leaves, chopped, plus more for garnish

1 Tbsp red pepper flakes

1–2 cups (8–16 oz/250–500 g) good-quality ricotta cheese, at room temperature

1 loaf good-quality ciabatta, thickly sliced

Good-quality thick aged balsamic vinegar (if not thick, reduce slightly)

Flaky sea salt, preferably Maldon, for garnish

This dish allows you to have a field day at the farmers' market. It was one of the first vegetarian-friendly recipes to go on the menu at Sorella and was an admission of sorts from Emma that vegetarians are not the enemy (a concept she had not previously been totally on board with). It's simple and delicious. Use avocado squash if you can find it, which is rich and creamy and does in fact resemble its namesake. A good-quality ricotta is key.

If you will be cooking the squashes on a charcoal grill, be sure to cut the slices large enough to keep them from falling through the grill rack. Build a hot fire in a charcoal grill and scrape the rack clean. Or, preheat a stove-top grill pan over high heat.

In a large bowl, toss the squash slices with a bit of kosher salt and just enough olive oil to coat. Let stand for a minute or so, then lift the slices out of the bowl, allowing any excess oil to drip off. Arrange the slices on the grill rack directly over the fire or on the grill pan. Let the squash slices sit quietly until they develop some color, then turn to grill the other side. (If you touch the slices before they have a nice char, they'll turn into a mushy mess.) In the same bowl, stir together the garlic, basil, and red pepper flakes. When the squash slices have nice grill marks on both sides and are slightly tender, transfer to the bowl with the garlic-basil mixture and toss gently to coat. Season with salt and a grind or two of pepper and stir to mix thoroughly. Set aside.

Brush a slice or two of ciabatta per diner with olive oil and add to the hot grill or grill pan. Grill, turning once, until nicely toasted.

to ASSEMBLE Place a dollop of ricotta on each piece of toast, spread thickly, and lay some warm squash on top. Arrange the toasts on a platter as you work. Garnish with more basil, a hefty drizzle of the balsamic, and a sprinkle of the sea salt and serve right away.

SARAH'S *drink note* This dish is summer specific and looks great with a glass of rosé. Because rosés come out in the late spring, they are nice and fresh in the summer. Try the Aglianico rosato from Taburno in Campania. It's a staple in my summer diet.

HOW WE HANDLE
CURDS

Mozzarella curd is the key ingredient for making fresh mozzarella, *stracciatella,* and, the badass combo of both, *burrata.* (Note the 'a' at the end of the word mozzarella and know now and forever that it is not silent.)

Mozzarella is made by softening the curd in hot salted water, then hand pulling it until smooth. *Stracciatella*, which means to tear apart, is made by breaking down the curd into strands and then mixing them with heavy cream. *Burrata* is a shell of pulled fresh mozzarella that is then stuffed with *stracciatella.*

These three cheeses hail from Puglia in southern Italy and are available here as imports. They are expensive and have a very short shelf life. Making them at home is a better, and obviously more fun, option. Mozzarella curd can be found in Italian specialty stores or online.

. . . .

HOMEMADE STRACCIATELLA

MAKES ABOUT 2 QT (2 L)

2 cups (12 oz/375 g) mozzarella curd

Kosher salt

2 cups (16 fl oz/500 ml) heavy cream, preferably from a local farm, plus more if desired

Like most clever delights in Italy, *stracciatella* was created by using the leftover scraps when making mozzarella. Start by grating the mozzarella curd into strands on the medium holes of a box grater. Using your hands, toss together the strands in a bowl. Add a hefty pinch of salt (see note), then slowly add the cream, stirring with your hands until a puddinglike consistency forms. Keep in mind that this mixture will get thicker as it sits, and you can always add more cream later if you need to thin it out. Place the mixture in an airtight container and refrigerate. It should stay good for up to 7 days, but it won't last that long because you'll eat it sooner.

Note: Salt can be intimidating. Remember you can always add salt, but you can't take it away. Tasting your food is the only way to learn how to season properly.

Sourcing good cream from a farm instead of using an ultra pasteurized product will ensure a better result.

PÂTÉ DI FEGATO

SERVES 6–8

In the early days, this pâté was a mascot of sorts for Sorella. It was shameless and beautiful and caused guests to inadvertently reach for their hearts as they read the ingredients. It is still not for the faint of heart, so, seriously, if you have a heart condition, sit this one out.

FOR *the* SUGARED BACON

1 lb (500 g) high-quality slab bacon, cut into ½-inch (12-mm) lardons

¼ cup (2 oz/60 g) sugar

½ tsp kosher salt

FOR *the* PÂTÉ

3 Tbsp extra-virgin olive oil

1 lb (500 g) chicken livers, cleaned and patted dry

¼ cup (2 fl oz/60 ml) rendered bacon fat

1 red onion, thinly sliced (about 1 cup/3½ oz/105 g)

2 cloves garlic, chopped

3 oil-packed anchovy fillets

3 Tbsp brine-packed capers

2 Tbsp tomato paste

1 cup (8 fl oz/250 ml) dry red wine

¼ cup (2 fl oz/60 ml) red wine vinegar

3 Tbsp kosher salt

½ cup (4 oz/125 g) cold unsalted butter, cut into small cubes

1 cup (8 fl oz/250 ml) heavy cream, whipped to medium peaks

FOR *each* PÂTÉ TOAST

1 tsp duck fat

1 slice English Muffin Bread, homemade (page 224) or store-bought, 1 inch (2.5 cm) thick

¼ cup (2 oz/60 g) pâté (above)

2 Tbsp sugared bacon (above)

1 egg, cooked sunny-side-up, trimmed with a 3-inch (7.5-cm) ring mold and seasoned with salt and freshly ground pepper

Chopped fresh flat-leaf parsley for garnish

To make the sugared bacon, in a sauté pan over medium-low heat, begin frying the bacon lardons until they are a little more than three-fourths of the way to being crisp and there is plenty of fat in the pan. Pour off the bacon fat into a heatproof cup and reserve. Add the sugar, salt, and ¼ cup (2 oz/60 ml) water to the pan. Cook, stirring to coat the bacon, until the liquid has reduced to a syrup. Remove from the heat and let cool. (The sugared bacon will keep in an airtight container in the refrigerator for up to 7 days.)

To make the pâté, in a large sauté pan over medium-high heat, warm the olive oil. When the oil is almost smoking, carefully put in the livers to sear. Cook for about 1 minute on each side. You want the livers to be cooked to medium-rare or barely medium. The more you cook livers, the more livery and chalky the taste gets. You do not want that taste here! Transfer the livers to a plate and set aside in a cool place.

In a rondeau or other wide, shallow pot, start heating the bacon fat over medium heat. Add the onion, garlic, anchovies, and capers. Sweat until the onion is translucent and the anchovies have begun to dissolve, 3–5 minutes. Add the tomato paste and cook until rust colored. Add the wine, vinegar, and salt and stir well to incorporate. Reduce the heat to low and simmer until a loose, ketchupy consistency forms. Remove from the heat and let the mixture cool to a little above room temperature.

Time to get the food processor out. In the work bowl, combine the livers and the wine mixture. With the machine running, slowly add the butter cubes. Process until thoroughly mixed and smooth.

Push the pâté through a tamis or fine-mesh sieve into a bowl to get the ultimate smooth consistency. Let cool completely. After it has cooled, very gently fold the whipped cream into the pâté just until no white streaks remain. Do not overmix. Taste and add more salt if needed, folding it in gently. Scrape the pâté into a container with a tight-fitting lid. (The pâté will keep in the refrigerator for up to 4 days.)

Following is how we assemble our pâté toasts at Sorella. The ingredients are broken down to 1 serving, so you can multiply as you like. Remember, the pâté will keep for up to 4 days, and the sugared bacon will last even longer.

to ASSEMBLE Smear the duck fat on the bread slice and grill or toast until golden. Let the bread cool slightly so the pâté does not melt when you are trying to spread it. (Think cream cheese on a hot bagel: if you smear it when the bagel is too hot, the cheese is just going to turn into a melted mess.) Quickly apply the pâté to the bread, touching it as little as possible. Sprinkle the bacon on top of the pâté. Top with the egg and sprinkle with parsley. Serve right away.

SPINACH
and
KALE DIP

with

ORANGE-WALNUT GREMOLATA

SERVES 6–10

3 Tbsp unsalted butter

3 shallots, thinly sliced

1 lb (500 g) spinach, stemmed

1 lb (500 g) kale, preferably black Tuscan, stemmed

Grated zest and juice of 1 lemon

Kosher salt and freshly ground pepper

3 oz (90 g) Parmesan cheese, grated

¼ cup (2 oz/60 g) crème fraîche

2 heaping Tbsp Dijon mustard

Pinch of red pepper flakes

FOR *the* GREMOLATA

2 Tbsp unsalted butter, at room temperature

3 cloves garlic, minced

½ cup (2 oz/60 g) plain dried bread crumbs

Kosher salt

½ cup (2 oz/60 g) walnuts, toasted and finely chopped

2 Tbsp grated orange zest

½ cup (½ oz/15 g) packed fresh flat-leaf parsley leaves, roughly chopped

Finely grated Parmesan cheese (preferably grated with a Microplane grater) for garnish

We are extremely fond of the flatbread we make at Sorella and are always looking for new ways to use it. Besides incessantly snacking on the crispy pieces, we discovered our flatbread is a great vessel for dipping. Everyone loves a dip, so we put a dip on the menu. When I dip, you dip, we dip... flatbread.

In a large sauté pan over medium heat, melt the butter. Add the shallots and sauté until golden in color and beginning to caramelize, about 5 minutes. Add the spinach and kale to the pan and allow them to wilt. Stir in the lemon zest and juice and some salt as the greens are wilting. You may need to add a bit of water too, depending on how tough your kale is. Use tongs to lift and turn the greens so they wilt evenly.

When the greens are completely wilted, transfer the mixture to a food processor. Wipe the pan clean and reserve. Add the cheese, crème fraîche, mustard, red pepper flakes, and a grind or two of black pepper to the food processor and process to a coarse purée. Taste the dip. You may need to add a little bit more lemon or salt to give it a yummy, rich pop. Scrape the dip into a baking dish or several small ramekins. Set aside.

Preheat the oven to 400°F (200°C).

To make the gremolata, in the reserved pan over medium heat, melt the butter. Add the garlic and bread crumbs and stir and toss to coat. Toast until the crumbs are a rich golden brown. Hit the mixture with some salt and remove from the heat. Toss in the walnuts, orange zest, and parsley. Set aside.

to ASSEMBLE Bake the dip until the edges are slightly browned and the juices are bubbling, about 20 minutes. About 4 minutes before it's done, top it with the gremolata and brown a bit more. Remove from the oven and let cool slightly, then garnish with a shower of snowy Parmesan and serve warm.

HEIRLOOM
TOMATO
SALAD
with
BAGNA CAUDA

SERVES 4–6

Bagna cauda is a traditional Piemontese hot dip typically served in the fall and winter. It is an intense fonduelike dish made with anchovies, garlic, butter, and sometimes cream. We wanted to make it into something lighter that could be eaten in the warmer months, too, so we turned it into a dressing for this simple salad. If you'd like to make your own rye bread, add a small handful of caraway seeds to the dough of our English Muffin Bread (page 224).

FOR *the* RYE CROUTONS

3 Tbsp unsalted butter

4 slices rye bread, crusts removed, cut into pea-size dice

Kosher salt

FOR *the* BAGNA CAUDA

½ cup (4 fl oz/125 ml) extra-virgin olive oil

2 Tbsp unsalted butter

8 oil-packed anchovy fillets

5 cloves garlic

20 cherry tomatoes, cut in half

6–8 heirloom tomatoes, in a mix of colors, cored and cut into slices and wedges

¼ cup (2 fl oz/60 ml) extra-virgin olive oil

¼ cup (2 fl oz/60 ml) red wine vinegar

Kosher salt and freshly ground pepper

½ cup (½ oz/15 g) packed fresh basil leaves, cut into chiffonade

Homemade Stracciatella (page 63) for serving

Flaky sea salt, preferably Maldon, for garnish

To make the croutons, in a sauté pan over medium heat, melt the butter. Add the bread and sauté until golden brown and crispy on all sides, about 4 minutes. Drain on a paper towel and season with kosher salt. Set aside to cool.

To make the bagna cauda, in a small saucepan over very low heat, combine the olive oil, butter, anchovies, and garlic. Warm the mixture, stirring occasionally, until the garlic softens and the anchovies break down, about 15 minutes. Transfer to a blender and blend to a smooth purée. Set aside.

Put all of the tomatoes in a large bowl, add the olive oil and vinegar, and season with kosher salt and pepper. Toss to mix and coat well. Seasoning is very important here—salt makes or breaks a tomato. Fold a bit of the basil into the dressed tomatoes.

to ASSEMBLE Arrange the tomatoes on large salad plates or a platter, adding tablespoon-size dollops of stracciatella along the way. The plate should begin to look like a pretty tomato Picasso. Drizzle the bagna cauda over the tomatoes and stracciatella. Garnish with the remaining basil and the croutons. Finish with a sprinkle of sea salt and a grind or two of black pepper.

ESCAROLE SALAD

with

HAZELNUTS *and* PECORINO

SERVES 4–6

1 small red onion, cut in half lengthwise and sliced very thinly

¾ cup (3½ oz/105 g) hazelnuts

2–3 heads escarole

5 oz (155 g) young pecorino cheese, preferably aged 3 months, grated

Kosher salt and freshly ground pepper

⅓ cup (3 fl oz/80 ml) extra-virgin olive oil

Juice of 1½ lemons

This was the first salad to go on the menu at Sorella. We added it because savvy New York food writer Andrea Strong told us we had to have a salad on our menu. At first, it came with a brown butter dressing. When we proudly showed Andrea the dish, her response was, "Are you serious? You finally have a salad and it comes with butter dressing?" So we changed it to lemon and olive oil and it's been that way ever since.

Immerse the onion slices in ice water to cover and refrigerate for at least 30 minutes or up to 5 hours to make them less pungent and to crisp them. Drain and shake off the excess water. Set aside.

Just before you take the onion out of the fridge, preheat the oven to 350°F (180°C). Spread the hazelnuts on a baking sheet and toast in the oven until the color darkens a little and the skins start to blister, 10–15 minutes. Pour the hot nuts onto a clean kitchen towel, gather up the corners, and let steam for 1 minute, then rub vigorously in the towel to remove the skins. Chop roughly and set aside.

Core the escarole and discard any discolored leaves. Cut the leaves into bite-size pieces. (You never want to present a bite that's too big; it's a symptom of an inconsiderate cook.) Wash the escarole and spin or pat dry thoroughly.

In a large bowl, combine the escarole, onion, hazelnuts, and pecorino. Season to taste with salt and pepper. Drizzle with the olive oil and lemon juice. Toss with your hands, being careful not to overmix. Taste. The salad should be light, lemony, and fresh, with the richness of nuts and cheese. Arrange on individual plates or a platter and serve right away.

SARAH'S *drink note* Don't outshine this simple salad with anything powerful. Go with a nice light, fresh white, like a Frascati.

KALE SALAD

and

SQUASHES, ALMONDS, *and* GRANA

SERVES 4–6

1 delicata squash

1 red kuri squash

8 Tbsp (4 fl oz/125 ml) extra-virgin olive oil

3 Tbsp fresh lemon juice, plus ¼ cup (2 fl oz/60 ml)

⅓ cup (4 fl oz/125 ml) honey

Kosher salt and freshly ground pepper

3 bunches Tuscan black kale, stemmed and cut crosswise into ½-inch (12-mm) chiffonade

1 cup (5½ oz/170 g) Marcona almonds, roughly chopped

¼ cup (1 oz/30 g) finely grated grana or Parmesan cheese (preferably grated with a Microplane grater)

Good-quality thick aged balsamic vinegar (if not thick, reduce slightly) for drizzling

1–2 oz (30–60 g) Podda Classico or Manchego cheese for shaving

We wanted to continue using fresh, seasonal produce throughout the fall, so we added this salad to the menu. Kale is one of our favorite things to eat. It has since become a celebrity in the vegetable world and can be found on many restaurant menus, but at the time it was really just an excuse to keep going to the Greenmarket. You can substitute any winter squash or pumpkin for the kuri.

Halve the delicata squash, scoop out and discard the seeds, and peel away the skin. Using a mandoline, slice the squash into paper-thin half-moons. (If you don't have a mandoline, use a vegetable peeler and make ribbons.) Set aside. Halve the kuri squash, scoop out and discard the seeds, and peel away the skin. Cut the flesh into ¾-inch (2-cm) dice.

Heat a large sauté pan over high heat and add 3 Tbsp of the olive oil. When the oil is almost smoking, add the kuri squash. Cook, turning as needed, until golden on all sides. Don't touch the pieces too much; you want the squash to develop a caramel color. Turn down the heat to medium, add the 3 Tbsp lemon juice and the honey, and stir to help the honey melt. Season the squash with a little salt and pepper at this point. Cook, stirring gently a few times, until the liquid is reduced to a glaze coating the squash. Set aside.

to ASSEMBLE In a large bowl, combine the cooked squash, raw squash, kale, and almonds. Toss all of this with the ¼ cup (2 fl oz/60 ml) lemon juice, the remaining 5 Tbsp (2½ fl oz/75 ml) olive oil, and the grana. Massage the dressing into the kale, being careful not to smoosh the cooked squash too much. Season with more salt and pepper.

Pile the salad on a platter or individual plates and drizzle the balsamic over the top. Shave a hefty dose of the Podda Classico over the top to add richness to the salad. Serve right away.

sarah's drink note We typically eat this salad during the colder months, but I still like a white wine with it. Try a richer varietal, such as Erbaluce. The creaminess of the wine pairs well with the sweet squash.

BROCCOLI FRITTO

SERVES 4–6

We call this the brocc-o-mole, because if you look around Sorella during service, it's on every table. It has garnered lots of fans and can outshine a main course: spicy, cheesy, fried, it fills the room with a great scent. If you have a lingering childhood animosity toward vegetables, this is the dish that will set you free.

Vegetable oil for deep-frying

FOR *the* **BATTER**

2 cups (11 oz/345 g) rice flour

1 Tbsp kosher salt

1 cup (8 fl oz/250 ml) ice water

1 lb (500 g) broccoli, trimmed and cut into florets

Kosher salt

Pickled Pepper Aioli (page 231)

½ cup (½ oz/15 g) packed fresh basil leaves, cut into chiffonade

½ cup (2 oz/60 g) grana or Parmesan cheese, finely grated (preferably grated with a Microplane grater)

Before you do anything, pour oil into a saucepan or deep fryer to a depth of 4 inches (10 cm) and heat over high heat to 360°F (185°C). You want an ample, stable pot of oil to work with.

To make the batter, in a large bowl, whisk together the rice flour and salt. Add the ice water slowly while stirring with your fingers. Lumps are just fine; they will fall off the florets. You do not want to overmix this. The final consistency should be heavy and wet like that of sludgy clay.

Get ready to fry the florets in batches. It is of the utmost importance that you do not crowd the broccoli in the pan. Place a handful of the florets in the batter and mix with your hands until fully coated. Using your hands, lift the florets out of the batter. Place the battered florets in the hot oil and cook for about 1½ minutes. They shouldn't necessarily color. We are not looking for a golden brown finish here. The trick to rice flour batters like this one or the type used for tempura is to fry the battered items just until the batter crisps up and becomes a thin, light, glassy shell. Using a slotted spoon or a wire skimmer, transfer to paper towels to drain. Repeat to fry the remaining broccoli, continuing to be careful not to crowd the florets in the pot and letting the oil return to 360°F (185°C) between batches.

to **ASSEMBLE** Place the florets in a large bowl and toss them with salt like you would French fries. Spread the salted florets in a single layer on a serving platter or plates and drizzle a good amount of the aioli on top, like covering fries with ketchup. Sprinkle the basil on top of the aioli and top that with a snowy layer of cheese. Enjoy immensely—and watch your guests freak out when they taste it.

RADISH

and

FENNEL SALAD

with GOAT'S MILK BUTTER, TORN HERBS, *and* ORANGE GASTRIQUE

SERVES 6–8

This salad is a play on the classic French combo of radishes and butter. Radishes seem to come in an infinite array of shapes, colors, and sizes. Use as many types as you can find and cut them all differently. A good finishing salt makes this pretty salad memorable.

FOR *the* COMPOUND GOAT'S MILK BUTTER

1 cup (8 oz/250 g) goat's milk butter, at room temperature

1 Tbsp extra-virgin olive oil

1 tsp flaky sea salt, preferably Maldon

FOR *the* GASTRIQUE

1 cup (8 fl oz/250 ml) fresh orange juice

½ cup (4 fl oz/125 ml) fresh lemon juice

¼ cup (2 oz/60 g) sugar

1 tsp peppercorns

1½ Tbsp rice vinegar

Pinch of kosher salt

1½ lb (750 g) mixed radishes, any combination, trimmed then cut and sliced in various ways

2 fennel bulbs, trimmed, cored, and very thinly shaved

½ cup (½ oz/15 g) packed fresh basil leaves, torn into small pieces, plus a bit more for garnish

½ cup (½ oz/15 g) packed fresh dill sprigs, torn into small pieces, plus a bit more for garnish

Extra-virgin olive oil for drizzling

Flaky sea salt, preferably Maldon

To make the compound butter, in a small bowl, combine the goat's milk butter, olive oil, and sea salt and beat until well mixed and airy, about 2 minutes. Set aside at room temperature until ready to serve.

To make the gastrique, in a saucepan over medium-high heat, whisk together the orange juice, lemon juice, sugar, peppercorns, vinegar, and kosher salt and bring to a boil. Reduce the heat to medium and simmer, stirring occasionally, until the mixture thickens enough to coat the back of a spoon, about 4 minutes. Remove from the heat. Strain the gastrique into a heatproof bowl or pitcher and set aside.

to ASSEMBLE In a large bowl, combine the radishes, fennel, basil, and dill and toss to mix. Drizzle with some gastrique and olive oil. Season with sea salt. Make a swoosh of the seasoned compound butter on the bottom of individual salad bowls or plates or a large serving plate and pile the radish mixture on top. Garnish with a few more torn herbs. Drizzle with more gastrique, sprinkle with a little salt, and serve right away.

SHAVED BRUSSELS SPROUTS SALAD

with CHARRED RED ONION

SERVES 4–6

Here is Emma's favorite salad on the planet. It's salty, earthy, spicy, and creamy. It's also delicious. Basically, it is what happens when Thai food and Italian food collide in the mind of a cook.

FOR *the* DRESSING

⅓ cup (3 fl oz/90 ml) extra-virgin olive oil

¼ cup (2 fl oz/60 ml) rice vinegar

3 Tbsp fresh lemon juice

¼ cup (2 fl oz/60 ml) sambal oelek, or to taste

FOR *the* RYE CROUTONS

3 Tbsp unsalted butter

3 slices rye bread, crusts removed, cut into pea-size dice

Kosher salt

2 lb (1 kg) Brussels sprouts, trimmed

1 red onion, cut into thick slices

½ cup (3 oz/90 g) dried currants, rehydrated in warm water, drained, and patted dry

¼ cup (⅓ oz/10 g) finely chopped fresh mint

Kosher salt

Homemade Stracciatella (page 63) for serving

To make the dressing, in a bowl, whisk together the olive oil, vinegar, lemon juice, and sambal. Depending on your heat tolerance, you may want to adjust the amount of sambal. Set aside.

To make the croutons, in a sauté pan over medium heat, melt the butter. Add the bread cubes and sauté until golden brown and crispy on all sides, about 4 minutes. Drain on a paper towel and season with salt. Set aside.

Using a mandoline or a sharp chef's knife, cut the Brussels sprouts lengthwise into thin slices, about ⅛ inch (3 mm) thick. Set aside.

Build a hot fire in a charcoal grill. Scrape the rack clean and brush lightly with oil. (You can also char the onion on a well-oiled stove-top grill pan preheated over high heat.) Arrange the onion slices on the grill rack directly over the fire and grill, turning once, until softened and nicely etched with grill marks. Transfer to a cutting board and let cool slightly, then chop roughly and set aside.

to ASSEMBLE Combine the Brussels sprouts, onion, currants, mint, and all but a small handful of the croutons in a large bowl and toss to mix. Add the dressing and toss again, then season with a bit of salt. On a serving plate, spread a little of the salad and top with a dollop or two of the stracciatella. Repeat the layers at least twice, until you have a pretty mound of salad. Garnish with the remaining croutons and serve right away.

SARAH'S *drink note* I like to drink a slightly off-dry wine with this salad because of the spice. If you enjoy Rieslings but not the syrupy ones, try a Kerner instead. The Kofererhof Kerner is killer.

BEET SALAD

with

HONEYED RICOTTA, PISTACHIOS, *and* KALE CHIPS

SERVES 4–6

Nearly every New York City restaurant has its version of beet salad. We originally made ours with beets, *tonnato* sauce, veal tongue, and pulled hen. Although it was really good, it proved to be a little too unique for our guests. So we tweaked the dish a bit, added some ricotta, and it flew out of the kitchen.

15 or so baby candy-cane-striped or golden beets, trimmed and scrubbed

3 or 4 large red beets, trimmed and scrubbed

2 or 3 fennel bulbs

FOR *the* HONEYED RICOTTA

1 cup (8 oz/250 g) ricotta cheese

¼ cup (3 fl oz/90 g) honey

1 Tbsp extra-virgin olive oil

Kosher salt and freshly ground pepper

FOR *the* PICKLED BEET PURÉE

½ cup (4 oz/125 g) pickled beets and a bit of the pickling liquid (see page 232)

2 Tbsp extra-virgin olive oil

FOR *the* KALE CHIPS

Vegetable oil for deep-frying

1 Tbsp fennel pollen

1 Tbsp kosher salt

1 bunch kale, stemmed and cut into 1-inch (2.5-cm) squares

¾ cup (3 oz/90 g) pistachios, toasted and chopped

¼ cup (2 fl oz/60 ml) fresh lemon juice

2 Tbsp fresh orange juice

⅓ cup (3 fl oz/80 ml) extra-virgin olive oil, plus more for drizzling

Kosher salt

Boil or roast (at about 375°F/190°C) the small and large beets separately until fork-tender. The timing will vary depending on the size of the beets and how fresh they are; start checking each at 20 minutes. Let cool slightly. Peel the beets by rubbing with paper towels. Rinse gently. Quarter the small beets and cut the large ones into bite-size chunks. Set aside.

Cut off the stalks and feathery tops from the fennel bulbs. (Discard them, or save for stock.) Cut the bulbs in half and cut away the core. Shave the fennel paper-thin on a mandoline or slice very thinly with a sharp chef's knife. Place in a bowl of ice water. Set aside.

To make the honeyed ricotta, in a small bowl, combine the ricotta, honey, olive oil, and salt and pepper to taste. Whip until fluffy and shiny. Set aside at room temperature.

Make the pickled beets as directed. In a blender, combine the pickled beets and olive oil and blend to a smooth purée. Thin out with a bit of pickling liquid if needed; the purée should be the consistency of a thin ketchup. Transfer the purée to a plastic squeeze bottle.

To make the kale chips, pour oil into a medium saucepan or deep-fryer to a depth of 2 inches (5 cm) and heat over high heat to 360°F (185°C). In a small bowl, stir together the fennel pollen and salt.

A handful at a time, add the kale pieces to the hot oil and fry until crispy. Using a skimmer or slotted spoon, transfer to paper towels to drain. Season with the salt mixture while still warm.

to ASSEMBLE In a large bowl, toss the beets, fennel, and most of the pistachios with the lemon and orange juices and the olive oil. Season with salt.

Apply a hefty smear of ricotta on the bottom of a platter or individual plates. Pile the beet and fennel mixture on top of the ricotta and dot with the beet purée. Garnish with the kale chips, a few more pistachios, and a drizzle of oil. Serve right away.

FAVA
and
PEA SALAD

SERVES 4–6

This is the perfect early spring salad. The ingredients become available right at the end of winter when you couldn't possibly eat another squash and are starting to crave sweet, green vegetables. At Sorella, we serve our flatbread (page 223) on top of this salad, adding some roasted garlic to the dough for extra kick.

FOR *the* CANDIED LEMON ZEST

1 lemon

¼ cup (2 oz/60 g) sugar

2 serrano chiles

1 red onion, thickly sliced and rings kept intact

½ cup (4 fl oz/125 ml) extra-virgin olive oil

2 Tbsp rice vinegar

1 Tbsp fresh orange juice

Pinch of grated orange zest

Pinch of salt

2 cups (10 oz/315 g) shelled fava beans

4 cups (1¼ lb/625 g) sugar snap peas

2 cups (10 oz/315 g) shelled English peas

⅓ cup (3 fl oz/80 ml) extra-virgin olive oil

2 Tbsp chopped fresh mint

Kosher salt and freshly ground pepper (optional)

Homemade Stracciatella (page 63) for serving

To make the candied zest, scrub the lemon thoroughly. Remove the zest with a vegetable peeler, being careful to remove only the bright yellow part and not the white pith underneath. Cut the zest into julienne. In a small saucepan, combine the lemon zest, sugar, and ⅓ cup (3 fl oz/80 ml) water. Cook over medium heat until most of the water evaporates and the liquid is syrupy, about 7–10 minutes. The zest should become tender and a bit translucent. Remove from the heat and let cool. Set the zest aside in its syrup.

Build a hot fire in a charcoal grill. Scrape the rack clean and brush lightly with oil. (You can also char the chiles and red onion on a well-oiled stove-top grill pan preheated over high heat or directly on your burner.)

To roast the chiles for the dressing, arrange them on the grill rack directly over the fire and grill, turning a few times, until the skins are nicely charred on all sides, about 10 minutes. Transfer to a plate to cool.

Arrange the onion slices on the hot grill and grill, turning once, until softened and nicely etched with grill marks, about 3 minutes per side. Transfer to a cutting board and let cool slightly, then chop and set aside.

To finish the dressing, in a food processor, combine the grilled chiles, the ½ cup (4 fl oz/125 ml) olive oil, the vinegar, orange juice and zest, and the salt. Pulse to a pulpy consistency. Set aside.

Bring a saucepan of heavily salted water to a boil over high heat. Set a large bowl of ice water nearby. Add the fava beans to the boiling water and cook until tender, about 2 minutes. Using a slotted spoon, transfer to the ice water to stop the cooking. Add the sugar snap peas to the boiling water and cook until tender, about 1 minute. Meanwhile, scoop the fava beans out of the ice water. When the sugar snap peas are ready, use the slotted spoon to transfer the snap peas to the ice water to stop the cooking. Pinch or peel the tough inner skins off the fava beans and set aside in a bowl. Drain the sugar snap peas, pat dry, and add to the favas. Set aside.

In a food processor, combine the English peas and ⅓ cup (3 fl oz/80 ml) olive oil and pulse just until evenly smashed. The peas should still be quite chunky. (This can also be done with a mortar and pestle.)

***to* ASSEMBLE** In a large bowl, toss together the favas, snap peas, smashed peas, grilled onion, mint, and dressing. Taste and adjust the seasoning with some pepper or extra salt, if you wish. Plate with a dollop of the stracciatella and garnish with the candied lemon zest, using a fork or your fingers to pluck pieces from the syrup and drape on the salad. Serve right away.

ARUGULA

and

PROSCIUTTO SALAD

with PICKLED PEARS
and ROASTED PEAR
VINAIGRETTE

SERVES 4–6

A Sorella staple, this salad is always made with a cured meat, a seasonal green, and a fresh or pickled fruit. It originally went on the menu with sugar plums or Italian plums, but since then we've made it with everything from figs to Concord grapes to pears.

FOR *the* DRESSING

2 ripe pears, peeled, halved, cored, and chopped

⅓ cup (3 fl oz/80 ml) rice vinegar

Grated zest and juice of ½ orange

1 Tbsp sugar

1 tsp crushed pink peppercorns

1 cup (8 fl oz/250 ml) grapeseed oil

Kosher salt

12–15 slices prosciutto di Parma

½ lb (250 g) arugula, preferably baby

1 cup (4 oz/125 g) pickled pears (see page 232)

½ cup (2 oz/60 g) sunflower seeds, toasted

¼ lb (125 g) Podda Classico cheese, shaved with a vegetable peeler

Preheat the oven to 375°F (190°C).

To make the dressing, spread the pears on a baking sheet and roast until the juices are bubbling, about 30 minutes. Transfer to a blender and add the vinegar, orange zest and juice, sugar, and peppercorns. Turn the blender to medium speed and slowly drizzle in the oil. Blend until emulsified. Finish with a pinch of salt. Set aside.

to **ASSEMBLE** Lay the prosciutto slices on a serving plate to create a bed for the salad. In a large bowl, toss together the arugula, pickled pears, and all but a couple tablespoons of the sunflower seeds with some of the dressing, being careful not to overdress. Mound the dressed salad on top of the prosciutto and top with the cheese. Sprinkle with the reserved sunflower seeds and serve right away.

GRILLED
CORN
SALAD

with

CHILE-LIME DRESSING *and* CORN BREAD CROUTONS

SERVES 4–6

FOR *the* DRESSING

¾ cup (6 oz/185 g) crème fraîche

2 Tbsp extra-virgin olive oil

Grated zest and juice of 2 large limes

1 Tbsp chile powder

½ tsp cayenne pepper

1 Tbsp sugar

Kosher salt

A few thick slices corn bread, store-bought or your favorite homemade

4 ears fresh corn

3 or 4 heads Little Gem or Bibb lettuce, cored and torn into large pieces

10 oz (315 g) ricotta salata cheese, shredded

1 cup (1 oz/30 g) packed fresh basil leaves, cut into chiffonade

¼ lb (125 g) grana cheese, finely grated (preferably grated with a Microplane grater)

Sometimes you just want a salad with a bunch of stuff on it. If Mexican street corn and a salad bar met and had a beautiful and sophisticated daughter, this would be her. The chile-lime dressing becomes truly fantastic if it sits in the refrigerator for a day or two.

To make the dressing, in a bowl, whisk together the crème fraîche, olive oil, lime zest and juice, chile powder, cayenne pepper, sugar, and salt to taste. Cover and refrigerate for at least 20 minutes or preferably overnight.

Preheat the oven to 200°F (95°C). Put the corn bread in a single layer on a baking sheet and place in the oven to dry out, about 15 minutes. Let cool, then break up into small croutons.

Build a hot fire in a charcoal grill. Scrape the rack clean and brush lightly with oil. (You can also char the corn on a well-oiled stove-top grill pan preheated over medium heat.) Husk the corn and remove the silk. Arrange the corn directly over the hot fire and grill, turning a few times, until lightly etched with grill marks all over and tender-crisp.

Remove the corn from the grill and let the ears cool until you can handle them, then cut the kernels off the cobs. Scrape the cobs with the back of a knife to release the excess corn flesh and the milk.

to ASSEMBLE In a large bowl, combine the lettuce, grilled corn, ricotta salata, basil, and cornbread croutons. Toss with enough of the dressing to coat thoroughly; this salad should be dressed like a creamy Caesar salad. Plate the salad in a high pile and top with a snowy layer of the grana. Serve right away.

WATERMELON and CUCUMBER SALAD

—— *with* ——

GOAT CHEESE and SWEET SHALLOTS

◆—— SERVES 4–6 ——◆

"Put a cashew on it!" This was our philosophy at Sorella for a long time. We are cashew addicts, and we ate this salad nearly every day that it was on the menu. Eventually our iron and zinc levels were off the charts and we had to take the salad off, but it still holds a special place in our hearts. It's an especially refreshing and reviving salad for the dead heat of summer.

FOR *the* GOAT CHEESE

6 oz (185 g) fresh goat cheese, at room temperature

¼ cup (2 fl oz/60 ml) extra-virgin olive oil

Pinch of kosher salt

FOR *the* SWEET SHALLOTS

⅓ cup (1½ oz/45 g) thinly sliced shallots

1 Tbsp rice vinegar

1 Tbsp sugar

2 lb (1 kg) ripe, seedless watermelon, rind removed and flesh cut into 1-inch (2.5-cm) cubes

2 large cucumbers, peeled, seeded, and cut into ½-inch (12-mm) cubes

½ cup (½ oz/15 g) packed fresh basil leaves, cut into chiffonade

1 cup (5½ oz/170 g) cashews, toasted and coarsely chopped

2 Tbsp fresh lemon juice

2 Tbsp rice vinegar

⅓ cup (3 fl oz/80 ml) extra-virgin olive oil, plus more for drizzling

Kosher salt and freshly ground pepper

In a bowl, combine the goat cheese, olive oil, and a pinch of salt and whip vigorously until well mixed and fluffy. Set aside.

In a small bowl, toss together the shallots, 1 Tbsp rice vinegar, and the sugar until the shallots are well coated. Set aside.

to ASSEMBLE In a large bowl, combine the watermelon, cucumbers, half of the basil, half of the cashews, and half of the shallots. Add the lemon juice, 2 Tbsp rice vinegar, and the olive oil and toss to coat. Season with salt and a hefty dose of pepper and toss again gently to mix. Pile the salad on a platter or individual plates and dot generously with the whipped goat cheese. Garnish with the remaining basil, cashews, and shallots. Drizzle with a little more olive oil and serve right away.

LAMB TONGUE

with BLACK LENTIL, CARAMELIZED SHALLOT, *and* ARTICHOKE CONFIT

SERVES 4–6

Ain't nothing scary about a little tongue! This dish features the ultra tasty combo of curry and artichokes, and the lentils add great texture. Using black lentils is important, as they hold their shape well. You will need to plan ahead for this recipe: the lamb tongues must sit in the brine for a day or two, then rest in the braising liquid overnight.

FOR *the* LAMB TONGUE

1 cup (8 oz/250 g) sugar

½ cup (4 oz/125 g) salt

3 cloves garlic, smashed

1 tsp caraway seeds

1 tsp whole cloves

1 tsp whole allspice

4–6 spring lamb tongues

10 baby artichokes, prickly tips, stems, and tough outer leaves removed

Extra-virgin olive oil as needed

2 cups (14 oz/440 g) black lentils

12 Tbsp (6 oz/185 g) unsalted butter

8 shallots, thinly sliced

Kosher salt and freshly ground pepper

2 cloves garlic, thinly sliced

Grated zest and juice of ½ lemon

Grated zest and juice of ½ orange

½ cup (½ oz/15 g) packed fresh flat-leaf parsley leaves, roughly chopped

1½ cups (12 fl oz/375 ml) Curry Aioli (page 230)

To prepare the lamb tongue, in a large saucepan, combine the sugar, salt, garlic, caraway seeds, cloves, allspice, and 4 cups (32 fl oz/1 l) water. Bring to a simmer over medium-high heat, stirring to dissolve the salt and sugar, then remove from the heat and let cool to room temperature. Add the lamb tongues to the brine. Place a plate on top of the tongues to keep them submerged. Cover and refrigerate for 24–48 hours.

Preheat the oven to 225°F (110°C).

Transfer the tongues to a Dutch oven or rondeau and pour in the brine. Add 1 cup (8 fl oz/250 ml) water to dilute the brine a bit. Cover tightly and place in the oven. Braise until very tender, about 4 hours. Remove from the oven and let cool in the braising liquid at room temperature overnight. Remove the tongues from the liquid, reserving the liquid. Peel off the skin from the tongues and remove any veins and bits of fat. Cut the tongues into ¼-inch (6-mm) dice. Set aside.

Pack the artichokes in a small saucepan, add olive oil to cover, and place over medium-low heat. Poach gently until tender, 30–40 minutes. Remove from the heat and set the artichokes aside in their oil.

While the artichokes are cooking, put the lentils in a saucepan with cold water to cover amply and bring to a boil over medium-high heat. Reduce the heat to medium and simmer until tender, about 45 minutes. Drain well and set aside.

Melt 4 Tbsp (2 oz/60 g) of the butter in a small frying pan over medium heat and add the shallots. Cook slowly until golden brown, about 6 minutes. Season with salt and a bit of pepper. Set aside.

Divide the remaining 8 tablespoons (4 oz/125 g) butter between 2 sauté pans. Place 1 pan over medium heat and melt the butter. Add the diced lamb tongue and sauté until lightly browned. Add the garlic and cook for 1 minute. Add a large pinch of the orange and lemon zests and a squeeze of each juice, followed by a splash of the reserved braising liquid. Cook until the sauce reduces to a shiny glaze that coats the lamb tongues. Taste and adjust the seasoning.

Melt the butter in the second pan over medium heat. Remove the artichokes from the oil and, using your hands, break them up into the pan. Add the cooked lentils and caramelized shallots, stir well to mix everything with the butter, and heat through. Toss in the parsley and a tiny bit of water to emulsify the sauce. Taste and season.

to **ASSEMBLE** Make a swoosh of the aioli on the bottom half of each plate. Place a spoonful of the lentil mixture above the aioli. Spoon the tongue on top of the lentils. Drizzle with the glaze remaining in the lamb tongue pan and serve right away.

CRISPY
VEAL
SWEETBREADS *with*
DIPPING SAUCES

➤ SERVES 4–6 ◆

3½ cups (28 fl oz/875 ml)
whole milk

Scant ¼ cup (2 oz/60 g) kosher salt,
plus more for seasoning

¼ cup (2 oz/60 g) sugar

2 lb (1 kg) veal sweetbreads

Vegetable oil for deep-frying

2 cups (11 oz/345 g) Cream of Wheat

2 cups (6 oz/185 g) graham
cracker crumbs

Sweet-and-Sour Lilikoi (page 230),
Barker's Mustard (page 230),
and/or Quince and Bacon Marmalade
(page 230) for dipping

Affectionately referred to as Gland McNuggets, this dish first appeared on the menu with our Quince and Bacon Marmalade. We soon realized that changing the dipping sauce created a whole different experience, so we played around. Plus, nuggets are best with a variety of dipping sauces. The breading is good on anything.

In a saucepan over medium heat, combine the milk, salt, and sugar and bring to a gentle boil, stirring to dissolve the salt and sugar. Add the sweetbreads, reduce the heat to maintain a low simmer, and poach the sweetbreads until they are about 85 percent cooked and their exterior is slightly firm, about 20 minutes.

Drain the sweetbreads and place them on a plate. Lay a clean kitchen towel on top and place another plate directly on top of that. Place a heavy can of beans or something of similar weight on the top plate. Transfer the whole setup to the refrigerator to press and chill, about 2 hours.

When the sweetbreads are cold and compressed to about half their height, you can go ahead and clean them. Remove all of the tissue around each piece and break them up into 1½-inch (4-cm) nuggets. Put them in a bowl of cold water and set aside.

Pour oil into a medium saucepan or deep fryer to a depth of 2 inches (5 cm) and heat over high heat to 360°F (185°C).

While the oil is heating, in a bowl, whisk together the Cream of Wheat and graham cracker crumbs to make the breading. Take the sweetbread nuggets out of the water and shake off the excess liquid. Put the nuggets in the breading and toss to coat, pressing firmly on the breading to help it adhere.

Working in batches, add the nuggets to the hot oil and fry until golden brown, about 6 minutes. Using a slotted spoon or wire skimmer, transfer to paper towels to drain. Toss the nuggets with salt as you would French fries. Serve warm, with the dipping sauce(s) of your choice.

SARAH'S *drink note* The rich, fatty gaminess of this dish goes well with bubbles. Try something extra dry, like Franciacorta.

WARM SHERRIED
MUSHROOM SALAD

with

HIJIKI *and*
PINE NUT PURÉE

SERVES 4–6

This salad came along during a phase of Asian persuasion at Sorella. We wanted something that was earthy and warm and not at all sweet. The result is an umami bomb. You can find *hijiki* in Asian markets, health-food stores, or online.

FOR *the* PINE NUT PURÉE

2 cups (10 oz/315 g) pine nuts, toasted until golden

1 Tbsp mirin

Pinch of sugar

Pinch of kosher salt

FOR *the* SHERRY DRESSING

1 large shallot, minced

1 Tbsp extra-virgin olive oil

1 cup (8 fl oz/250 ml) sherry

¼ cup (2 fl oz/60 ml) sherry vinegar

Pinch of grated orange zest

¼ cup (2 fl oz/60 ml) extra-virgin olive oil

2 cups (6 oz/185 g) stemmed and sliced shiitake mushrooms

2 cups (6 oz/185 g) stemmed and sliced oyster or maitake mushrooms

2 cups (6 oz/185 g) stemmed and sliced chanterelle mushrooms

6 Tbsp (3 oz/90 g) unsalted butter

Kosher salt

4–6 Tokyo turnips, trimmed and very thinly sliced on a mandoline or with a sharp chef's knife

½ cup (3 oz/90 g) dried hijiki, soaked in warm water and drained

Pinch of grated lemon zest

1 cup (6 oz/185 g) pickled honshimeji mushrooms (see page 232)

½ cup (½ oz/15 g) packed fresh flat-leaf parsley leaves

To make the pine nut purée, in a small saucepan, combine 1½ cups (7½ oz/235 g) of the pine nuts with 1 cup (8 fl oz/250 ml) water, the mirin, sugar, and salt. Cook over low heat, stirring, until the nuts start to take on a soft and translucent appearance, about 10 minutes. Remove from the heat and let cool slightly, then transfer to a blender and blend to a very creamy purée. It should have the texture of a shiny, smooth, creamy peanut butter. Set aside. Reserve the rest of the pine nuts for garnish.

To make the dressing, in a small saucepan over medium heat, sweat the shallot in the olive oil. After a minute or so, add the sherry and reduce by about half. Remove from the heat and add the vinegar and orange zest while still warm. Cover to keep warm and set aside.

In a very large sauté pan over medium-high heat, warm the extra-virgin olive oil until almost smoking. Add the mushrooms, a small handful at a time. Don't touch or shake them right away. Allow them to cook and caramelize a bit until brown and crispy, about 2 minutes. Add the butter after the mushrooms have some color and stir to help it melt. Cook until the butter is browned and the mushrooms are brown and crispy, 3–5 minutes. Season liberally with salt and scrape into a large bowl. While still warm, mix the mushrooms with the turnips, hijiki, and lemon zest, then gradually stir in the warm dressing.

to ASSEMBLE Make a swoosh of the pine nut purée on a platter or individual plates. Top with the warm mushroom salad. Garnish with the pickled mushrooms, the reserved pine nuts, and the parsley. Serve right away.

STUFFED ONION

with

FONDUTA, AMARETTI, *and* SAGE

SERVES 6–8

We first tried this unique and traditional dish at the original Slow Food-designated restaurant in Alba during the annual truffle festival. The onion arrived covered with white truffles and sitting atop a Barolo leaf. That was a really hard day.

6–8 medium yellow onions

FOR *the* FILLING

2 Tbsp olive oil

3 oz (90 g) pancetta, diced

½ lb (250 g) ground veal

½ cup (3 oz/90 g) golden raisins, chopped

¼ cup (½ oz/15 g) chopped fresh sage

½ cup (½ oz/15 g) chopped fresh flat-leaf parsley leaves

1 Tbsp chopped fresh thyme

Grated zest and juice of ½ orange and ½ lemon

¼ tsp *each* ground allspice, ground cloves, and freshly grated nutmeg

½ cup (4 fl oz/125 ml) *each* dark rum and heavy cream

1 cup (4 oz/125 g) fine dried bread crumbs

Kosher salt

1 large egg, beaten

FOR *the* FONDUTA

1 Tbsp *each* unsalted butter and all-purpose flour

1 cup (8 fl oz/250 ml) whole milk

½ tsp freshly grated nutmeg

3 oz (90 g) fontina cheese, shredded

¼ cup (1 oz/30 g) freshly grated Parmesan cheese

Kosher salt and freshly ground pepper

1 cup (4 oz/125 g) amaretti cookies, broken up into pieces

1 large white truffle (optional)

6–8 sage leaves, fried

Preheat the oven to 325°F (165°C). Cut off the top one-fourth of the blossom end of each onion. Then cut a thin slice off the root end so the onions will stand upright. Place the onions on a roasting rack set over a baking sheet and replace the tops. Roast until soft, 45–60 minutes. Give the onions a squeeze with tongs. If the inside layers squeeze out a bit and are soft, the onions are done. Let cool slightly on the rack. Set the tops aside again and gently squeeze out a few of the inside layers of the onions onto a cutting board. Be careful to keep 2 or 3 thick outer layers of each onion intact to ensure a sturdy shell for stuffing. Return the shells to the rack on the baking sheet, standing them upright. Have the tops nearby. Chop the inner portions of the onions and transfer to a bowl for the filling. Set aside.

To make the filling, drizzle the olive oil into a pot, add the pancetta, and fry over medium heat to render the fat, stirring occasionally. When the pancetta is translucent, add the veal. Brown off the veal, breaking it up with a spoon. Add the reserved chopped onion, raisins, sage, parsley, thyme, orange and lemon zest and juice, allspice, cloves, and nutmeg and stir to mix well.

Stir in the rum, scraping up any browned bits from the pan bottom. Simmer until reduced by half. Add the cream and reduce again until the mixture is quite thick. Make sure it does not scorch. Remove from the heat and fold in the bread crumbs. Let cool to room temperature. This is the perfect time to taste and season liberally with kosher salt. Add the egg and mix thoroughly. The stuffing should have the consistency of a slightly wet meatball.

Raise the oven temperature to 400°F (200°C).

Using a teaspoon or soupspoon, stuff each onion with the filling until the cavity is full. Transfer them to the rack on the baking sheet. Replace the tops and slide the sheet into the oven. Bake until the stuffed onions are hot throughout, about 15 minutes.

Meanwhile, make the fonduta: In a medium saucepan over low heat, melt the butter. Whisk in the flour until well blended. Add the milk and continue to whisk until the mixture thickens slightly. Add the nutmeg and cheeses and continue whisking until the cheeses have melted and the sauce is thick, about 10 minutes. Season with a hefty pinch of salt and a few grinds of pepper and remove from the heat. Let cool slightly, then transfer to a plastic squeeze bottle.

to ASSEMBLE When the onions are hot, remove from the oven, take off the tops, and immediately squeeze about 2 Tbsp of the fonduta into the filling in each onion using the tip of the squeeze bottle. Sprinkle a pinch or two of the amaretti crumbs on top. Use the remaining amaretti crumbs to make a bed on a platter or on individual plates. Nestle the onions upright in the crumbs. If you have a truffle, use a grater to shower the onions with thin slices of truffle in front of your guests. Top with the fried sage leaves and serve right away.

UN PO DI PASTA

Gnudi with Summer Corn and Torn Herbs 100

Chestnut Stracci with Braised Pork, Molasses Brown Butter, and Sage 103

White Rabbit Bolognese Lasagne 107

Mezze Maniche with Hot Sausage, Avocado Squash, and Padrón Peppers 108

Pici with Pork Ragù, Ricotta, and Pepperoncini 113

Orecchiette with Braised Duck, Broccoli Rabe, Peanuts, and Cilantro 114

The Sorella Gnocchi 119

Maltagliati with White Beans, Guanciale, and Crispy Carrots 123

Tajarin with Lamb Ragù, Black Pepper Ricotta, Pistachios, and Mint 126

Agnolotti dal Plin 131

Spring Garlic Spaghetti Carbonara 132

Sweet Potato Tortelli with Hot Cacciatorini and Maple Brown Butter 133

Spicy Shrimp Risotto 136

Braised Oxtail Risotto 138

Risotto with Porcini Ragù 139

It's no secret that pasta, the source of most people's affinity for Italian food, is a crowd-pleaser. Everybody loves it, and we are no different. In fact, we love it to almost a dangerous degree. Although making fresh pasta can be a lot of work and messy, it can also be a lot of fun when you get the hang of it. If you cannot make it at home, do not fret. Plenty of excellent-quality dried pastas are on the market. It's easy to make pasta dishes appropriate for any occasion. On a cold night, for example, you can warm up with a hearty *ragù* tossed with hand-cut *pici*. In summer, you can go lighter with a sauce of fresh corn kernels and torn herbs. Running a marathon? That's the world's best excuse for eating a mountain of pasta. Here are some of the pastas that have graced the menu at Sorella. Some are staples, some come and go, but all are favorites and all are delicious.

GNUDI

with

SUMMER CORN *and* TORN HERBS

—◆— SERVES 4–6 —◆—

Gnudi are essentially naked ravioli. It's important to use a dry ricotta when making this recipe or the *gnudi* will be gummy (trust us, no one likes gummy *gnudi*). If the ricotta is particularly wet, hang it in cheesecloth to drain overnight. We serve this dish in late summer when fresh corn is at its sweetest.

FOR *the* GNUDI DOUGH

2 cups (1 lb/500 g) whole-milk ricotta cheese

1 large egg

1 cup (4½ oz/140 g) 00 flour, plus about 2 cups (9 oz/280 g) for rolling

1 tsp kosher salt

½ tsp freshly ground pepper

6–8 ears fresh corn

1 bay leaf

2 Tbsp sugar

4 Tbsp (2 oz/60 g) unsalted butter, at room temperature

Kosher salt and freshly ground pepper

1 heaping cup (generous 1 oz/30 g) mixed fresh herb leaves, preferably including basil, tarragon, mint, marjoram, dill, flat-leaf parsley, and chives, torn by hand

½ cup (2 oz/60 g) finely grated Parmesan cheese (preferably grated with a Microplane grater)

To make the dough, in a large bowl, combine the ricotta, egg, 1 cup flour, salt, and pepper and stir just until blended. Knead briefly in the bowl just until a soft dough forms. It is important that the dough not develop too much gluten. If it does, you will have a gluey mess.

Put the 2 cups flour in a large shallow bowl and set nearby. Pick off small pieces of dough from the mound and roll each one into a ball about the size of a giant gumball or slightly smaller than a golf ball. Toss the balls in the flour, coating them completely. Store the gnudi in the flour in the refrigerator until ready to use.

Husk the corn and remove the silk. Cut the kernels off the cobs and reserve. Using the back of a knife, scrape the cobs over a large pot to release the excess corn flesh and the milk. Snap the cobs into pieces and drop them into the pot. Add the bay leaf, sugar, and 2 qt (2 l) water. Simmer over medium heat, stirring once in a while until a delicious corn stock develops, about 45 minutes. Remove from the heat. Strain the stock and reserve.

In a large sauté pan, bring about 1½ cups (12 fl oz/375 ml) of the corn stock to a simmer. Remove the gnudi from the bowl of flour, shaking off the excess flour, and add them to the pan. The stock should come about halfway up the sides of the gnudi. Add more stock or pour off some as needed. Return to a simmer and cook, shaking the pan a few times and rolling the gnudi around gently to make sure they cook evenly. Continue simmering until the liquid is reduced to about ½ cup (4 fl oz/125 ml), about 3 minutes. At this point, the gnudi should be cooked through. To test, cut into one; it should be doughy on the outside but softer inside. Add the reserved corn kernels and butter to make a sauce and season with salt and pepper. Cook until the sauce coats the gnudi like shiny velvet, about 2 minutes longer.

To serve, divide the gnudi among pasta bowls or plates and drizzle with some of the sauce remaining in the pot. Top with the torn herbs, sprinkle with the cheese, and serve right away.

SARAH'S *drink note* A lot of work and love go into making gnudi. Keep the wine choice light, with a sparkling rosé or a slightly off-dry sparkling wine. The sparkling Kerner from Carpenè Malvolti is a great choice.

CHESTNUT STRACCI

with

BRAISED PORK, MOLASSES BROWN BUTTER, *and* SAGE

SERVES 4–6

For the first six weeks that we were open, the menu at Sorella consisted of a mix of *qualcosina*, some sides, meat, and cheese. Guests were often confused. "You don't have any main courses?" they would ask. So we launched a weekly changing menu of three larger dishes. This was the first pasta on that menu (*stracci* is Italian for "rags"). It's rich and wintry and superfilling. For the best results, plan to start the pork a day in advance so it can sit in its braising liquid overnight.

FOR *the* BRAISED PORK

1 yellow onion, chopped

1 carrot, peeled and chopped

2 ribs celery, chopped

3 cloves garlic, chopped

1 orange, quartered

1 cup (8 fl oz/250 ml) dry white wine

1 cup (8 fl oz/250 ml) apple juice

1 cup (8 fl oz/250 ml) whole milk

1 bay leaf

A few fresh thyme sprigs

A sprinkle of peppercorns

A handful of coarse salt

1½ lb (750 g) boneless pork butt (pork shoulder), trimmed of excess fat and cut into small pieces

FOR *the* CHESTNUT STRACCI

1¾ cups (8 oz/250 g) 00 flour, plus more for rolling

1 cup (3½ oz/105 g) chestnut flour

Pinch of kosher salt

3 large eggs

1½ Tbsp extra-virgin olive oil

Ingredients continued

Preheat the oven to 225°F (110°C).

To make the braised pork, in a large roasting pan, combine the onion, carrot, celery, garlic, orange, wine, apple juice, milk, bay leaf, thyme, peppercorns, and salt and mix well. Add the pork butt and turn to coat in the liquid. Spread out the rest of the ingredients in the pan to distribute them evenly. Cover tightly with aluminum foil and braise until the pork meat is falling apart, 2–3 hours. Remove from the oven and let cool in the braising liquid to room temperature, then refrigerate overnight.

To make the stracci, in the bowl of a stand mixer, whisk or stir together the flours and salt. Make a well in the flour. In a small bowl, whisk together the eggs and olive olive until blended, then pour into the well in the flour. Fit the mixer with the dough hook, turn on the mixer to the lowest speed, and mix until the flours and egg mixture combine together in a rough mass. Increase the speed to medium-low and knead the dough until it is smooth and elastic. The whole kneading process should take about 20 minutes. Alternatively, to make the dough by hand, stir together the flours and salt in a large bowl. Make a well in the center, and pour the egg mixture into the well. Using a fork, gradually pull the flour into the egg mixture in the well. Continue to mix this way until a rough, shaggy dough forms. Lightly flour a work surface with 00 flour, and turn the dough out onto the floured surface. Knead until smooth and elastic, about 20 minutes. Let the dough rest in a covered bowl at room temperature for about 30 minutes. While the dough is resting, return the pork to a 225°F (110°C) oven to warm.

Divide the dough into 4 equal pieces. Lightly dust a large work surface with 00 flour. Using a pasta machine, roll out each piece of dough as thinly as possible, beginning with the widest setting on the machine and ending with the narrowest setting. Lightly dust your hands, the rollers, and the dough with flour as needed to prevent sticking as you work. Lay the pasta sheets flat on the floured surface. Leave the sheets to dry slightly while you pull the pork and prepare the braising jus. Then, using a fluted pasta wheel, cut the pasta sheets into strips about 3 inches (7.5 cm) long by 1½ inches (4 cm) wide. They do not need to be perfect!

Recipe method continued

Vegetable oil for frying

½ cup (4 oz/125 g) unsalted butter,
at room temperature,
plus more for finishing

2½ Tbsp molasses

10 or so fresh sage leaves

Kosher salt

Grated grana or Parmesan cheese
for serving

To pull the pork, remove the roasting pan from the oven and transfer the pork to a cutting board. Using 2 forks, pull the pork into pieces, then chop it up slightly. Set aside. (If the pork butt you bought has skin on it, save the skin to make pork rinds!) Pour the braising liquid with the vegetables into a pot and bring to a simmer over medium heat. Remove and discard the bay leaf, thyme sprigs, and orange. Using a handheld mixer, blend the vegetables into the liquid. Continue to simmer until the liquid has reduced enough to coat the back of a spoon, about 15 minutes. Remove from the heat, strain through a fine-mesh sieve into a small saucepan, and season with salt and pepper. Discard the solids. Cover the braising jus to keep warm.

Bring a large pot of heavily salted water to a boil. Pour vegetable oil to a depth of 1 inch (2.5 cm) into a small saucepan and heat to 360°F (185°C).

While the water and oil are heating, in a large sauté pan, melt the butter over medium heat. When the butter begins to bubble and foam, keep a close eye on it. Keep browning, stirring often, until it is a deep amber. Remove from the heat and let cool, then whisk with the molasses until fluffy and shiny. Set aside.

Pick out 4–6 of the prettiest sage leaves for garnish and toss them into the hot oil. Fry until the leaves are silent in the oil after the initial sizzle. Transfer to a paper towel to drain. Sprinkle with salt. Roughly chop the remaining sage and set aside.

Return the sauté pan with the molasses butter to medium heat. When the butter is hot, add the chopped sage and cook for a moment. Add the pulled pork and toss to coat. Add the braising jus and stir to emulsify with the butter. Begin to reduce.

Add the stracci to the boiling water and cook until tender, about 3 minutes. Drain, transfer to the sauté pan with the braised pork, and toss to mix. Taste and adjust the seasoning. Stir in a tiny bit more butter if needed to give the dish a nice sheen.

To serve, divide among pasta bowls or plates and scatter a generous amount of cheese on top. Garnish with the fried sage leaves and serve right away.

WHITE RABBIT
BOLOGNESE LASAGNE

SERVES 6–8

Lasagne in Italy is traditionally made with seven to ten very thin layers, and is much less sauce driven than what is served in the States. The pasta is an important part of this dish, and you should be able to taste it. You can substitute ground pork for the rabbit.

FOR *the* BOLOGNESE SAUCE

3 Tbsp extra-virgin olive oil

6 oz (185 g) guanciale or pancetta, cut into small dice

½ small fennel bulb, cored and cut into small dice

1 small leek, white and tender green parts, cut into small dice

½ yellow onion, cut into small dice

1 rib celery, cut into small dice

3 cloves garlic, minced

2 lb (1 kg) ground rabbit

1 cup (8 fl oz/250 ml) dry white wine

2 cups (16 fl oz/500 ml) whole milk

¼ cup (1 oz/30 g) walnuts, ground to a paste

Grated zest and juice of 1 lemon

Grated zest and juice of ½ orange

2 Tbsp coarsely chopped fresh sage

1 tsp dried thyme

1 bay leaf

¼ tsp ground cinnamon

¼ tsp ground allspice

4 tsp kosher salt

Semolina Pasta Dough (page 120)

FOR *the* BÉCHAMEL SAUCE

2 Tbsp unsalted butter

½ yellow onion, chopped

2 Tbsp all-purpose flour

2 cups (16 fl oz/500 ml) whole milk

Pinch of freshly grated nutmeg

Kosher salt and freshly ground pepper

Chopped fresh flat-leaf parsley for garnish

¼ lb (125 g) Parmesan cheese, grated

To make the Bolognese sauce, in a large saucepan over medium heat, warm the olive oil. Add the guanciale and fry until the fat renders and the pork is translucent, 5–8 minutes. Add the fennel, leek, onion, celery, and garlic and sweat for about 3 minutes. Add the rabbit and brown off, breaking up the meat with a whisk or spoon.

Add the wine and stir to scrape up any browned bits from the pan bottom. Simmer to reduce for a minute or so. Add the milk and walnut paste and give a stir. Add the lemon and orange zest and juice, sage, thyme, bay leaf, cinnamon, and allspice. Give another stir, partially cover, and reduce the heat to low. Simmer gently, stirring occasionally, until nicely thickened, about 1 hour. Stir in the salt. Taste and adjust the seasoning.

While the sauce is simmering, make the pasta dough as directed and let rest for 30 minutes. Divide the dough into 4 equal pieces. Lightly dust a large work surface with semolina flour. Using a pasta machine, roll out each piece of dough as thinly as possible, beginning with the widest setting on the machine and ending with the narrowest setting. Lightly dust your hands, the rollers, and the dough with flour as needed to prevent sticking as you work. As the pasta sheets become longer and thinner, they can be difficult to handle without tearing. If this should happen, cut the sheets in half crosswise to make them more manageable to feed through the rollers of the pasta machine. Lay the pasta sheets flat on the floured surface and let dry slightly while you make the béchamel sauce.

To make the béchamel sauce, in a saucepan over low heat, melt the butter, add the onion, and cook, stirring, until translucent but not browned, about 5 minutes. Whisk in the flour until well blended and cook, stirring, for a minute or two. Slowly whisk in the milk and continue to whisk until the mixture thickens slightly. Add the nutmeg and salt and pepper to taste. Strain through a fine-mesh sieve into a bowl and set aside.

Preheat the oven to 350°F (180°C).

to ASSEMBLE Grease a 9-by-13-inch (23-by-33-cm) baking pan with a bit of butter. Bring a pot of heavily salted water to a boil and, working in batches if necessary, gently cook the pasta sheets for 1 minute (they won't be quite tender yet), then drain in a colander, rinse with cold water, and drain again. In a large bowl, gently toss the cooked pasta sheets with a little olive oil to prevent sticking.

Place 1 or more pasta sheets on the bottom as needed to cover. Top with a scoop of the Bolognese sauce and then a scoop of the béchamel. Spread the sauces in an even layer and sprinkle a bit of Parmesan on top. Repeat these steps until you have 7–10 layers, saving a little béchamel and cheese for the top. Eyeball your sauces and cheese to divide them more or less evenly between layers, depending on how many pasta sheets you have. Do not put too much filling in each layer. This lasagne should be light, balanced, and delicate on the palate.

When you have finished making your layers, top with the reserved béchamel and half of the reserved Parmesan. Bake until the lasagne is set, the top is lightly browned, and the juices are bubbling, about 25 minutes. Remove from the oven and let cool for 10 minutes. Cut into squares and serve, garnished with the parsley and more Parmesan.

MEZZE MANICHE

with

HOT SAUSAGE, AVOCADO SQUASH, *and* PADRÓN PEPPERS

SERVES 6–8

This is a delicious and simple summer pasta that begs to be eaten outdoors. Padrón peppers, a Spanish cousin of the *shishito*, add a smoky, salty element to this seasonal dish. The avocado squash, developed in Asia and shaped a bit like its namesake, has a pleasant, nutty flavor and cooks quickly. You can substitute zucchini or any long squash.

Kosher salt and freshly ground pepper

1 lb (500 g) hot Italian sausage

1 avocado squash, cut into thin, bite-size pieces

½ lb (250 g) padrón peppers, roughly chopped

1 small bunch garlic chives, cut into very small dice

1½ lb (750 g) dried tubular pasta such as mezze maniche or rigatoni, or orecchiette

½ cup (4 oz/125 g) unsalted butter, at room temperature, cut into 4 or 5 pieces

6–8 oz (185–250 g) young pecorino cheese, grated

Bring a large pot of heavily salted water to a boil.

Meanwhile, crumble the sausages out of their casings into a wide saucepan over medium heat. Brown off the sausage until cooked through, 15–20 minutes. Add the squash, peppers, and all but about 2 Tbsp of the chives and sauté in the sausage fat for a minute or two, until the squash and peppers soften slightly.

Add the pasta to the boiling water and cook until al dente, following the package directions. Drain, reserving 1 cup (8 fl oz/250 ml) or so of the cooking water. Add the pasta to the sausage mixture along with a little of the reserved cooking water and the butter. When the butter has melted, stir until the sauce emulsifies and is clinging to the pasta. Add another splash of the pasta water if the mixture seems dry, or cook a little longer to reduce, if needed. Fold in all but a few tablespoons of the cheese and season with salt and pepper to taste.

Divide among pasta bowls or plates and garnish with the reserved cheese and chives. Serve right away.

SARAH'S *drink note* This pasta is pretty spicy. Cool off your palate with a crisp white from northern Italy, such as a Pinot Grigio.

HOW WE MAKE
PICI

Pici, which hail from the province of Siena, are thick, hand-rolled noodles that look like chubby spaghetti. We first ate them in the town of Montalcino while waiting out a storm. They are called *pinci* there, and they were dressed with pesto. On a sunny afternoon elsewhere in Tuscany, we ate them again, this time dressed with wild boar *ragù*. They have a wonderfully chewy and rustic texture and we love them.

The dough is typically made from just flour and water. Some recipes call for egg, but we keep it simple. With only two ingredients, the choice of flour is key. We use 00 and semolina for the best bite. That simplicity also makes it easy to know when the *pici* are done.

PICI

MAKES ABOUT 1 LB (500 G)

2 cups (9 oz/280 g) 00 flour, plus more for rolling

1 cup (5½ oz/170 g) semolina flour, plus more for rolling

1 Tbsp kosher salt

1½ cups (12 fl oz/375 ml) water

In the bowl of a stand mixer, whisk or stir together the flours and salt. Make a well in the mixture, and slowly pour water into the well. Fit the mixer with the dough hook, then turn on the mixer to the lowest speed and mix until the flours and water come together in a smooth, stiff ball. Increase the speed to medium-low and knead the dough until it is smooth and elastic, 4–6 minutes longer. Alternatively, to make the dough by hand, stir together the flours and salt in a large bowl. Make a well in the center, and pour in the water. Using a fork, gradually pull the flour into the well, then stir with a wood spoon until a rough, shaggy dough forms. Lightly flour a work surface with 00 flour, and turn the dough out onto the floured surface. Knead until smooth and elastic, 10–12 minutes. Let the dough rest in a covered bowl at room temperature for about 2 hours. This is a good time to make a ragù or other long-cooking sauce. (You can also make the dough a day ahead and let it rest overnight in the refrigerator. Let it warm at room temperature slightly before continuing.)

Uncover the dough and slice off a piece about as big as your hand. Lightly flour a work surface with semolina flour, place the piece on the floured surface, and flatten it with your hand into a rectangular strip roughly 2 inches (5 cm) wide. The exact width is not important. Cut the rectangle crosswise into wormlike strips. One at a time, using your palms, roll each strip back and forth on the work surface, starting in the middle and working your way outward until you have a rope about the thickness of a pencil. Don't worry about making the ropes uniform. This is not a fancy dinner-party pasta. Think rustic and homemade. Then, holding one end in each hand, gently stretch each rope. As you shape the noodles, toss them in 00 flour so they won't stick to anything or to one another, then spread them out on a baking sheet. Repeat until you have shaped all of the dough. If making this pasta seems oddly easy, that's because it is.

Let the pasta dry until slightly leathery, about 30 minutes. To store the pasta, cover tightly or slip into a resealable plastic bag, and refrigerate overnight. To freeze, spread the noodles out so they are not touching one another too much—a little contact is okay, as they will separate once they hit the boiling water—and freeze for up to 2 weeks.

Cook the pasta in salted boiling water. The noodles will be ready in 3–4 minutes. If they are undercooked, they will taste like raw flour and feel gummy in your mouth and the texture won't be nearly as fun as we promised.

PICI

with

PORK RAGÙ,

RICOTTA, *and*
PEPPERONCINI

SERVES 4–6

This was the last dish that Emma and Molly, our first sous chef, created together before Molly left Sorella the first time. The pickled pepper and salami combo make the *pici* taste like hoagie pasta, and any pasta that also makes you feel like you're eating a sandwich is pretty much okay in our book. As with any pasta, the noodles should be coated with but not lost in the sauce. Adjust the amount to your liking.

FOR *the* PORK RAGÙ

2 Tbsp extra-virgin olive oil

1 head garlic, finely chopped

4 shallots, finely chopped

2 Tbsp red pepper flakes

1 lb (500 g) ground pork

¾ lb (375 g) hot cacciatorini or other spicy dry salami, thinly sliced, then cut into julienne

½ cup (4 oz/125 g) tomato paste

2 cups (16 fl oz/500 ml) dry white wine

2 cups (16 fl oz/500 ml) whole milk

½ cup (4 fl oz/125 ml) heavy cream

A few bay leaves

Kosher salt

6 Tbsp (3 oz/90 g) unsalted butter, at room temperature

½ cup (½ oz/15 g) fresh flat-leaf parsley leaves, coarsely chopped

Pepperoncini brine for splashing, plus 1½ cups (7½ oz/235 g) drained jarred pepperoncini, thinly sliced

1 batch Pici (page 111)

1–1½ cups (8–12 oz/250–375 g) whole-milk ricotta cheese, preferably small-batch

Chopped fresh basil, for garnish

Grated Parmesan cheese for serving

To make the ragù, in a large saucepan, start heating up the olive oil over medium heat. Add the garlic, shallots, and red pepper flakes and cook, stirring occasionally, until the shallots are translucent, about 5 minutes. Add the pork and cacciatorini and brown off the pork, breaking it up with a whisk or spoon. Stir in the tomato paste and cook until it turns rust colored. Pour in the wine and deglaze the pan, stirring to scrape up any browned bits from the pan bottom. Bring to a simmer and cook until reduced by about one-fourth. Add the milk, cream, and bay leaves and stir a few times to combine. Reduce the heat to low, cover, and simmer very gently, stirring occasionally, until the sauce has thickened into a luscious ragù, 1–1½ hours. Season with salt. When the sauce is ready, it should no longer taste of the wine. Remove and discard the bay leaves and skim the fat off the top.

Bring a large pot of heavily salted water to a boil. While the water is heating, in a large saucepan over medium-low heat, combine about two-thirds of the ragù if cooking for 4 people and all if for 6, the butter, and the parsley and stir until the butter is melted. (Store any remaining ragù in a covered container in the refrigerator for up to 3 days.) Add a splash of water and a splash of the pepperoncini brine to loosen the ragù a bit and stir to mix well.

Add the pici to the boiling water and cook until the strands are no longer doughy but are still chewy, about 3 minutes. Drain the pici and add to the sauce. Cook to reduce the sauce for a few more minutes, if needed, until it clings to the pasta.

To serve, smear ¼ cup (2 oz/60 g) of the ricotta on each dinner plate. Top with the pici. Garnish with a generous sprinkle of the sliced pepperoncini, basil and Parmesan and serve right away.

ORECCHIETTE

with

BRAISED DUCK,

BROCCOLI RABE,
PEANUTS, *and* CILANTRO

SERVES 4–6

This flavorful pasta is what happens when *pad Thai* and *pad see-ew* go on an extended Italian vacation together. The duck takes some advance preparation (one night to marinate and another to rest after braising), but the dish comes together quickly in the end. The sauce should cling and be present but not overwhelm the orecchiette.

FOR *the* BRAISED DUCK

1 yellow onion, chopped

1 large carrot, peeled and chopped

4 cloves garlic, chopped

1 large orange, quartered

1 lemon, quartered

¼ cup (1 oz/30 g) peeled and chopped fresh ginger

1 habanero chile, halved

1 cup (7 oz/220 g) firmly packed brown sugar

2 cups (16 fl oz/500 ml) whiskey

⅓ cup (3 fl oz/80 ml) shoyu or soy sauce

⅓ cup (3 fl oz/80 ml) rice vinegar

5 duck legs (about 4 lb/2 kg total weight)

2 bunches broccoli rabe, trimmed

Kosher salt and freshly ground pepper

1 lb (500 g) fresh or dried orecchiette

½ cup (4 oz/125 g) unsalted butter, at room temperature

1 cup (5 oz/155 g) unsalted roasted peanuts, chopped

½ lemon (optional)

½ cup (½ oz/15 g) packed fresh cilantro leaves

To make the braised duck, in a large roasting pan, combine the onion, carrot, garlic, orange, lemon, ginger, chile, brown sugar, whiskey, shoyu, and vinegar and mix well.

Add the duck legs and turn to coat in the liquid. Spread out the vegetables and fruits in the pan to distribute them evenly. Cover tightly with a lid or aluminum foil and marinate overnight in the refrigerator.

Preheat the oven to 225°F (110°C). Remove the pan of duck legs from the fridge to take the chill off.

Transfer the duck to the oven, still tightly covered, and braise until the duck meat is falling off the bones, about 3 hours. Remove from the oven and let cool in the braising liquid to room temperature, then refrigerate overnight.

Return the pan to a 225°F (110°C) oven to warm. When the duck and pan juices are warm, remove from the oven and transfer the duck legs to a cutting board. Pull the meat off the bones and chop roughly. Set aside. To make the sauce, strain the braising liquid through a fine-mesh sieve into a saucepan. Discard the solids from the roasting pan. Add the duck bones to the braising liquid and bring to a simmer over medium-high heat. Cook until reduced enough to coat the back of a spoon, about 20 minutes. Discard the bones. Cover to keep warm and set aside.

Bring a saucepan of heavily salted water to a boil. Set a bowl of ice water nearby. Add the broccoli rabe to the boiling water and blanch just until tender, about 3 minutes. Drain, then immediately plunge into the ice water to stop the cooking. When cooled, drain again, pat dry, and cut into bite-size pieces. Set aside.

Bring a large pot of heavily salted water to a boil. Add the orecchiette and cook until al dente, following the package directions.

Meanwhile, in a large sauté pan over medium heat, combine the sauce and the butter and cook until the butter has melted. Add the duck meat and stir to coat. Fold in the broccoli rabe and all but a few tablespoons of the peanuts. When the orecchiette is done, drain and add to the pan with the duck. Cook for a few more minutes, if needed; you want the sauce to cling to the pasta. Give the whole thing a taste and adjust the seasoning with salt and pepper. It might need a squeeze of lemon, too.

To serve, divide among pasta bowls or plates. Garnish with the cilantro leaves and a few more peanuts and serve right away.

HOW WE MAKE
GNOCCHI

Gnocchi falls into the dumpling category, but the Italian versions are, of course, very different from the dumplings found in Sorella's neighboring Chinatown restaurants. These little nuggets are made from potato, flour, and egg and, when fashioned properly, their texture is ethereal. Light and airy little pillows, they melt in your mouth rather than sit like heavy, dense rocks in your stomach. You may not nail the technique the first time, but that's okay. New things are often a little awkward in the beginning.

The Sorella Gnocchi (page 119) were inspired by an otherworldly dining experience we had in Emilia-Romagna, where we ate tiny gnocchi in a lovely cream sauce. Our gnocchi became a smaller version that continued to shrink over time. Eventually a guest asked Sarah why the gnocchi were so tiny. She thought for a minute, then answered, "our chef has tiny hands."

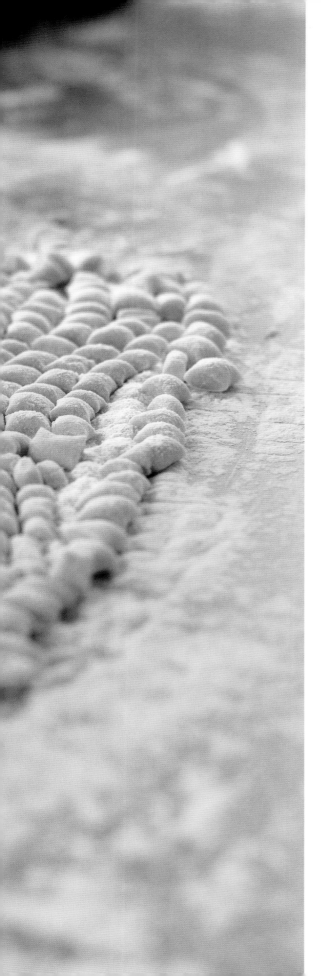

GNOCCHI

MAKES GNOCCHI FOR 8 AS AN APPETIZER
OR 4–6 FOR A MAIN COURSE

3 medium russet potatoes	2 Tbsp salt
1 whole large egg, plus 1 large egg white	½ cup (2 oz/60 g) flour, plus more for rolling and dusting

Starting with cold, unsalted water, boil the potatoes in their skins until knife tender but not falling apart. Drain the potatoes and put them on a tray until just cool enough to handle (if they sit in their skins too long, the potatoes will get gummy). Peel away the skins with your fingers, then pass the potatoes through a food mill fitted with a medium disk or a ricer held over a baking sheet. Spread out the potato bits to allow some heat and moisture to escape (if they cool in a big clump, the gnocchi will be gluey).

When the potatoes are still warm to the touch (about 110°F/43°C) but not piping hot, gently gather them in a mound and make a small well in the center. (The trick to good gnocchi is rolling the dough when it is at the right temperature.) The shape should recall a science-project volcano. Drop the whole egg and egg white, salt, and a handful of flour (about ¼ cup/1 oz/30 g) into the well. Using your fingertips, start to combine the ingredients by crumbling them together. Add another handful or so of flour and knead the dough just enough to form it into a ball. It should just hold together and feel firm yet yielding to the touch. Overmixing and too much flour are also culprits in creating heavy, gummy gnocchi.

Let the dough ball rest for 15–20 minutes. Do not let it sit too long, or it will deflate and become gluey. Press the ball with your fingertip. If it doesn't bounce back and the fingerprint remains, the dough is well rested. Cut off about one-third of the dough and place it on a clean work surface. Using your palms, roll the dough into a long, even rope about 1 inch (2.5 cm) in diameter. Cut the rope into 2 or 3 equal pieces. Working on a floured surface, roll each piece into a rope about ½ inch (12 mm) thick. When rolling, start in the middle and gradually move your hands out to the ends. Once you have made a few ropes, line them up horizontally and side by side and sprinkle flour on top. Using a clean, sharp knife, cut the ropes crosswise into pieces resembling mini marshmallows. Repeat with the remaining dough, making sure to clean your knife well after cutting each batch of ropes. Toss the tiny gnocchi around gently to make sure they are separate from one another and evenly coated with flour, then place them on a baking sheet and refrigerate uncovered until you are ready to cook them. They are best when eaten the day they are made, so if you want to eat them multiple times in a week, you'll get plenty of practice.

THE
SORELLA GNOCCHI

SERVES 4–6

In Piedmont, we ate teeny, tiny potato gnocchi everywhere we went. This recipe was inspired by an excellent version we had at Osteria dei Catari, in Monforte, where chef-owner Alessandro Cavallo topped gnocchi with sautéed pears and a cheesy cream sauce. Cut the pears the same size as the gnocchi, so they're camouflaged.

1 batch Gnocchi (page 117)

FOR *the* CASTELROSSO CHEESE SAUCE

1 shallot, thinly sliced

2 cloves garlic, thinly sliced

2 Tbsp extra-virgin olive oil

2 cups (16 fl oz/500 ml) heavy cream

½ lb (250 g) castelrosso or Humboldt Fog cheese, cut into 1-inch (2.5-cm) cubes with rind intact for stronger flavor

Kosher salt and freshly ground pepper

3 Tbsp unsalted butter

2 large, ripe but firm pears, peeled, halved, cored, and cut into tiny dice

Handful of chopped fresh chives for garnish

Make the gnocchi as directed and keep in the refrigerator until ready to cook.

To make the sauce, in a saucepan over medium heat, combine the shallot, garlic, and olive oil and sweat until softened, about 4 minutes. Do not allow to color. Pour in the cream and cook, stirring as needed to prevent scorching, until reduced by one-fourth, about 10 minutes.

Remove from the heat, add the cheese, and let sit for a minute to soften. Then, using a handheld blender or a stand blender, process the mixture until smooth and thick. Dip a spoon into the sauce, lift it out, and draw a fingertip along the back of the spoon. It should leave a clear trail. (The sauce will improve as it sits, so consider making it a day or two ahead. Leftover sauce will keep in an airtight container in the refrigerator for up to two days.)

Bring a large pot of salted water to a boil. Meanwhile, in a sauté pan over medium heat, combine the butter and pears and warm them together, shaking the pan occasionally. When they start to brown, add about 1 cup (8 fl oz/250 ml) water and deglaze the pan, stirring to dislodge any browned bits from the pan bottom. (Keep your face turned away when you add the water to avoid being burned by the hot steam.) Remove from the heat and shake the pan to color the pears evenly. Return the pan to medium heat and add about 1 cup (8 fl/250 ml) of the cheese sauce. Swirl the sauce in the pan and then start reducing the sauce. At the same time, drop your gnocchi into the boiling water. When the gnocchi start popping up, using a slotted spoon or wire skimmer, transfer them to the pan with the pears, reserving the cooking water. Continue reducing for 5–7 minutes. If the sauce breaks, add some of the gnocchi cooking water. Season with salt and pepper. The dish should be the consistency of gooey mac and cheese.

Divide the gnocchi among pasta bowls or plates. Top with the chives and serve right away.

SARAH'S *drink note* When I eat this dish in the fall, I always think of being in Piedmont, so I choose to drink Barbaresco. It's a good choice.

When dusting semolina pasta dough with flour, or working on a floured surface with semolina dough, only semolina flour should be used.

SEMOLINA PASTA DOUGH

MAKES 1 LB (500 G)

Our traditional pasta dough is made with all egg yolks to create a richer dough.

1 cup (4½ oz/140 g) 00 flour

½ cup (3 oz/90 g) semolina flour, plus more for the work surface

1 tsp kosher salt

10 large egg yolks

1 Tbsp extra-virgin olive oil

In a large bowl or the bowl of a stand mixer, whisk or beat together the flours and salt. Make a well in the flour. Add the eggs yolks, 2 Tbsp water, and the olive oil to the well and beat with a fork until well blended.

To make the dough by hand, using a fork, gradually pull the flour into the well, then stir with a wooden spoon until a rough, shaggy dough forms. Turn the dough out onto a lightly floured work surface and knead until smooth and elastic, about 20 minutes.

To make the dough in a stand mixer, fit the mixer with the dough hook and mix on low speed until a shaggy dough forms, then increase the speed to medium-low and knead until the dough is smooth and elastic, about 20 minutes.

Cover the dough with an overturned bowl and let rest for about 30 minutes if using right away, or wrap well and refrigerate for up to 2 days.

VARIATIONS

Tomato pasta dough: Replace the water with the same amount of puréed canned tomatoes.

Spinach pasta dough: Replace the water with the same amount of puréed blanched spinach.

Additional flavored doughs: Add 1 tablespoon of your choice of spice, seeds, or herbs (try ground caraway seeds, poppy seeds, or freshly ground pepper) to the dry ingredients.

MALTAGLIATI

with

WHITE BEANS, GUANCIALE, *and* CRISPY CARROTS

— SERVES 6–8 —

This is an old-school comfort dish from the lovely town of Modena, in Emilia-Romagna. It's what your mom would make you on a cold winter's day if you weren't feeling well—and your mom was a ninety-year-old Italian woman who wore a cute apron and didn't speak English. If matzo ball soup is the Jewish penicillin, this pasta is the Italian one. To save time, you can break up store-bought dried pasta for the fresh *maltagliati*.

FOR *the* BEANS

¾ cup (5 oz/155 g) dried white beans, picked over for grit and stones and soaked in cold water to cover overnight

1 qt (1 l) water or chicken stock

1 carrot, peeled and chopped

1 yellow onion, chopped

1 rib celery, chopped

2 cloves garlic, sliced

1 bay leaf

A hefty pinch of kosher salt

1 cup (8 fl oz/250 ml) dry white wine

1 batch Semolina Pasta Dough (page 120), or 1 lb (500 g) dried pasta sheets

Vegetable oil for deep-frying

1 lb (500 g) guanciale, cut into small dice

2 medium carrots, preferably heirloom, peeled and sliced into paper-thin rounds on a mandoline

Kosher salt and freshly ground pepper

2 cloves garlic, very thinly sliced

1–1½ tsp red pepper flakes

¼ cup (¼ oz/7 g) *each* chopped fresh rosemary, sage, and thyme

2 Tbsp (1 oz/30 g) unsalted butter, at room temperature

¼ cup (2 fl oz/60 ml) heavy cream

½ lemon

1 oz (30 g) *each* pecorino and Parmesan cheese, grated

Chopped fresh flat-leaf parsley for garnish

Drain the beans. Put them in a large pot and add the water or stock. Place the carrot, onion, celery, garlic, and bay leaf in a cheesecloth sachet, tie securely, and put in the pot with the beans. Throw in the salt and pour in the wine. Bring to a boil over high heat, then reduce the heat and simmer until the beans are extremely tender, almost to the point of falling apart, about 1¼–1½ hours. Remove from the heat and let the beans cool in the liquid. Discard the sachet.

While the beans are cooking, make the pasta dough as directed and let rest for 30 minutes. Lightly flour a work surface with semolina flour, and divide the dough in half for ease of rolling. Using a pasta machine, roll out each piece of dough as thinly as possible, beginning with the widest setting on the machine and ending with the narrowest setting. Then, using a fluted pasta wheel, cut the pasta sheets into shapes that more or less resemble trapezoids about 1 by 2 inches (2.5 by 5 cm). Let dry for about 10 minutes. If using dried pasta, break it into random pieces of about the same size. (The word maltagliati means "badly cut.")

Bring a large pot of salted water to a boil. Pour vegetable oil into a small, deep saucepan to a depth of about 1 inch (2.5 cm) and heat over high heat to 360°F (185°C).

While everything is heating, in a small frying pan over medium-low heat, slowly fry the guanciale until the fat is rendered and the pieces are crispy but still chewy, about 10 minutes. Using a slotted spoon, transfer the guanciale to paper towels to drain. Set aside the pan with the fat.

Working in batches, add the carrot slices to the hot vegetable oil and fry until lightly browned and crispy, about 2 minutes. Using a slotted spoon or a skimmer, transfer to paper towels to drain. (Alternatively, place in a dehydrator overnight until crispy.) Season with salt.

Add the pasta to the boiling water and cook just until about 80 percent done, about 2 minutes for fresh pasta or about 8 minutes for dried. Drain and set aside.

to ASSEMBLE Pour the reserved guanciale fat into a large sauté pan and place over medium heat. Add the garlic, red pepper flakes, rosemary, sage, and thyme and stir until fragrant, about 2 minutes. Add the beans and the guanciale and sauté or a minute or so longer. Add the cooked pasta and fold in the butter and cream. Cook until the sauce reduces and is clinging to the pasta, about 3 minutes. Squeeze in a splash of lemon juice. Fold in the cheeses, reserving a small handful. Season with salt and pepper.

Divide among pasta bowls or plates. Top with the crispy carrots, the parsley, and the reserved cheese. Serve right away.

HOW WE MAKE
TAJARIN

Tajarin, also known as *tagliolini*, is a thin, flat noodle from Piedmont. If you were born in Piedmont and female, chances are you were lucky enough to learn how to make *tajarin* as a little girl, which means you're now really cool. We make this noodle with our basic *pasta all'uovo* dough, which has all egg yolks, and a lot of them, which guarantees a richer dough, richer taste, and killer texture. In Italy, this pasta is typically rolled out and cut by hand. We can't pull that off at Sorella, so we use a pasta-dough sheeter and a special cutter we bought in Piedmont. We recommend you use a machine unless you want to be making *tajarin* for a week.

Make 1 batch Semolina Pasta Dough (page 120). Cut off a chunk of the dough and pass it through the pasta machine, starting at the widest setting and ending at the narrowest setting. The pasta sheet should be thin, but not so thin that if you held it up, you could see shadow puppets through it. Dust the sheet with semolina flour and pass it through a thin noodle cutter no more than $\frac{1}{16}$ inch (2 mm) wide. Toss the cut noodles to separate and uncurl them, then lay the strands on a baking sheet and cover with a kitchen towel so they don't get too dry.

When you cook fresh pasta rather than dried pasta, the bite is different. It won't be al dente, so don't think that you've overcooked the noodles. You also don't need crazy boiling water, which damages fresh pasta. It should be simmering.

We recommend eating this pasta toddler-style, with butter and Parmesan cheese. If you happen to have a white truffle on hand, shave it over the top for a mind-blowing finish.

TAJARIN

with

LAMB RAGÙ,

BLACK PEPPER RICOTTA, PISTACHIOS, *and* MINT

SERVES 6–8

When we were first developing this dish in our apartment, we had two versions of the *ragù*—one made with pulled lamb and the other made with ground lamb. We each fought hard for our preferred *ragù* but eventually the ground lamb one came out on top. The winner is hardly as important as how much people love this flavorful pasta. But also, it was Sarah.

FOR *the* LAMB RAGÙ

1 Tbsp extra-virgin olive oil

½ lb (250 g) pancetta, cut into small dice

1 yellow onion, cut into small dice

2 carrots, peeled and cut into small dice

2 ribs celery, cut into small dice

2 cloves garlic, minced

2 lb (1 kg) ground lamb

1 cup (8 oz/250 g) tomato paste

1 cup (8 fl oz/250 ml) dry white wine

1 cup (8 fl oz/250 ml) whole milk

4 Tbsp fennel seeds

2 Tbsp ground cardamom

1 orange, quartered

Kosher salt

1 batch Tajarin (page 125)

1½ cups (12 oz/375 g) whole-milk ricotta cheese

1 Tbsp freshly ground black pepper

1½ cups (6 oz/185 g) pistachios, coarsely chopped

1 cup (1 oz/30 g) packed fresh mint leaves, coarsely chopped

¼ cup (2 oz/60 g) unsalted butter, at room temperature, cut into 4 pieces

Grated Parmesan cheese for garnish

Chopped fresh flat-leaf parsley for garnish

To make the ragù, in a large saucepan, heat the olive oil over medium heat. Add the pancetta and fry until the fat is rendered and the pancetta is translucent, 5–8 minutes. Add the onion, carrots, celery, and garlic and sweat until the onion is translucent and the vegetables are soft, about 5 minutes. Add the lamb and brown it, breaking it up with a whisk or spoon.

Add the tomato paste and cook until it turns rust colored. Pour in the wine to deglaze the pan, stirring to scrape up any browned bits from the pan bottom. Simmer until reduced by about one-fourth. Add the milk, fennel seeds, cardamom, and orange and give the sauce a stir. Cover and reduce the heat so the sauce barely simmers. Cook, stirring occasionally, until thickened to a luscious ragù, about 1½ hours. Remove from the heat and let cool slightly. Skim off the fat, remove and discard the orange, and season with salt to taste. Set aside, or re-cover and refrigerate overnight.

When the sauce is about halfway done, make the tajarin as directed. Bring a large pot of heavily salted water to a boil. While the water is heating, get ready to assemble the dish: In a bowl, stir together the ricotta and black pepper and set aside. In a large sauté pan over low heat, combine about ⅓ cup (3 fl oz/80 ml) or so of the ragù per person with most of the pistachios and mint, reserving some of each. (Cover and store any leftover ragù in the fridge for up to 4 days.) Add a little water to loosen the ragù slightly.

to ASSEMBLE Add the tajarin to the simmering water and cook until about 80 percent done, about 2 minutes, giving the noodles a gentle stir in the pot once or twice with tongs. Drain the pasta and add it to the sauce in the pan. Then add the butter and stir to melt. Cook the sauce for a few more minutes, if needed, until it clings to the pasta.

To serve, divide among pasta bowls or plates and top with dollops of the black pepper ricotta. Garnish with the Parmesan, parsley, mint, and pistachios and serve right away.

HOW WE MAKE
AGNOLOTTI DAL PLIN

Agnolotti are a type of filled pasta made throughout Italy, but *agnolotti dal plin* are Piedmont specific. As it is the case with most regional specialities in Italy, the Piemontese swear their version is the best. We happen to agree. Our time in Alba coincided with the peak of white truffle season. In fact, we were there during the truffle festival, which is the best-smelling festival of all time. Every day during our stay we ate *agnolotti dal plin* with butter and white truffles for one or more meals. The name translates to "pinched pillows," and these little lovelies were a major contributor to our flesh being pinched by the buttons on our jeans due to our overeating.

At Sorella, we use our rich, eggy *pasta all'uovo* for the dough. Although *agnolotti dal plin* are hand shaped and may appear difficult, you'll get the hang of it quickly. Traditionally they are pretty tiny, about 1 inch (2.5 cm) in size. Finished, they look luxurious and dainty and will impress your guests.

....

Make 1 batch Semolina Pasta Dough (page 120). Cut off a big chunk of the dough and pass it through the pasta machine, starting at the widest setting and ending at the second-to-narrowest setting. Lay the sheet horizontally on a lightly floured work surface. Spoon marble-size balls of filling (page 131) along the edge closest to you, placing them about a thumb's distance away from one another and a fingertip in from the bottom edge. Fold the edge of the dough closest to you over the balls and press the edge down tightly. Using your fingers, pinch the dough upward between each filled pocket. With a fluted pasta cutter, trim away the pasta dough above the row of pockets. Press the seams tightly again.

Using the pasta cutter, roll over each upward pinch to release the agnolotti. As you cut and fill the agnolotti, place the filled pieces on lightly floured baking sheets. Repeat until you have used up the filling.

AGNOLOTTI

DAL PLIN

SERVES 4–6

Back in the day, the filling for these *agnolotti* was made from leftover roasted meat scraps. Here we use short ribs. Scatter a little Parm on top at serving if you like, but a cheese finish is not required for these rich purses of flavorful meat. A little shaved truffle would add a welcome earthy note.

FOR *the* FILLING

¼ cup (2 fl oz/60 ml) extra-virgin olive oil

2 lb (1 kg) boneless beef short ribs, trimmed, patted dry, and sprinkled generously with salt

3 cups (24 fl oz/750 ml) dry and pretty tasty red wine

2 Tbsp unsalted butter

2 or 3 shallots, chopped

4 cloves garlic, chopped

3 cups (9 oz/280 g) shredded green cabbage

¼ cup (¼ oz/7 g) packed fresh sage leaves, chopped

Grated zest and juice of 1 large lemon

1 tsp ground nutmeg

1½ tsp ground allspice

3 oz (90 g) Parmesan, grated (about ¾ cup)

3 Tbsp kosher salt

Freshly ground pepper

1 batch Semolina Pasta Dough (page 120)

5 Tbsp (2½ oz/75 g) unsalted butter

A few fresh sage leaves, torn

Grated Parmesan cheese for serving

Preheat the oven to 250°F (120°C).

To make the filling, in a large Dutch oven or rondeau, warm the olive oil over high heat until almost smoking. Add the short ribs and sear, turning as needed, until golden brown on all sides. Transfer to a plate and discard the oil. Return the short ribs to the pot and pour in the red wine. Cover, place in the oven, and braise until the meat is fork-tender, about 3 hours.

Remove from the oven. Using tongs, transfer the meat to a plate. Pour the liquid in the pot into a bowl and set aside. Place the pot over medium heat. Add the butter along with the shallots, garlic, and cabbage. Sweat until the shallots are translucent and the cabbage has wilted, 8–10 minutes, stirring to scrape up any browned bits from the pot bottom. Return the meat to the pot and break it up with the tongs. Add the chopped sage, lemon zest and juice, nutmeg, and allspice. Pour the cooking liquid back in and bring to a simmer. Cook for another 5 minutes or so. The filling should be neither soupy nor dry, just very juicy. If it gets too dry, add a little more red wine or water.

Take the filling mixture off the heat and get your food processor out. In the work bowl, combine the filling and the cheese and process until the mixture takes on a pastelike consistency. At this point, you are ready to season. Transfer to a bowl and stir in the salt and pepper to taste. Don't be shy with the salt. Work it in gradually, if you like, but the mixture should be on the verge of tasting salty. Before stuffing the agnolotti, cover and refrigerate the filling until it is cold. (The filling can be made ahead. Let cool completely, then scoop into resealable freezer bags and freeze for up to 2 weeks.) Make the pasta dough as directed.

***to* ASSEMBLE** Bring a large pot of heavily salted water to a boil. While the water is heating, cut and fill the agnolotti (see page 128), placing them on lightly floured baking sheets as they are finished.

In a sauté pan over medium heat, melt the butter with ¼ cup (2 fl oz/60 ml) water and the torn sage. Whisk to emulsify the water and butter into a sauce. Keep warm over low heat. Carefully put about half of the agnolotti in the gently boiling water and cook until they float to the top, about 2 minutes. Using a slotted spoon, transfer them to the sage butter and turn gently to coat. Repeat with the remaining agnolotti. Divide among pasta bowls or plates. Garnish with Parmesan and serve right away.

SPRING GARLIC
SPAGHETTI CARBONARA

SERVES 4

When I was accepted to the Culinary Institute of America, my dad bought me *The Professional Chef* cookbook that I needed for school and marked the page for carbonara. We lived in Key West, where the food was not exciting, and I'd never had carbonara. He said he wanted it to be the first thing I made for him after graduation. He passed away two days after I started school. I really wish he could have had the version that Emma and I serve at Sorella.

Kosher salt and freshly ground pepper

2 large whole eggs

2 large egg yolks

2 oz (60 g) pecorino romano cheese, finely grated (preferably grated with a Microplane grater), plus an extra chunk for garnish

1 bunch spring garlic, trimmed

Extra-virgin olive oil for sautéing

¼ lb (125 g) pancetta or guanciale, cut into small lardons

¾ lb (375 g) dried spaghetti

Get some water boiling with a bit of salt for your pasta. Don't make it too salty this time, because you are going to mix the pasta with some fairly salty stuff.

In a bowl, whisk together the whole eggs, egg yolks, grated cheese, and a bunch of cracked pepper. Set aside.

Using a mandoline or a sharp chef's knife, cut the garlic bulbs and some of the tender green parts into paper-thin slices. You want about 1 cup (5 oz/155 g). Set aside.

In a large sauté pan over medium heat, warm a drizzle of olive oil. Add the pancetta and fry until slightly crispy. Reserve a few pretty rings of the spring garlic for garnish and add the rest to the pan. Sauté until softened, a minute or two. Remove from the heat and keep warm.

While the pancetta is cooking, add the spaghetti to the boiling water and cook until al dente, 8–10 minutes. While the pasta is cooking, round up your guests, place them in their seats, and do not let them move. They must be prepared to eat this immediately or else all your work will go to waste. Using tongs, add the pasta to the sauté pan, reserving the cooking water.

Toss the pasta briefly with the pork and garlic, then add the egg and cheese mixture and quickly stir and toss to coat the pasta evenly. Thin with the pasta water as needed, adding just a splash at a time, until a creamy sauce forms. Divide among pasta bowls or plates and grate a little more cheese on top. Garnish with more cracked pepper and the reserved spring garlic rings. Serve and eat pronto.

SWEET POTATO
TORTELLI
with

HOT CACCIATORINI
and MAPLE BROWN
BUTTER

SERVES 4–6

Sweet potatoes are both delicious and nutritious. They are always in full swing around the fall and winter holidays, and this pasta is like a holiday party in your mouth. The combination may seem strange but it positively sings. It's sweet, salty, spicy, and rich.

1 batch Semolina Pasta Dough
(page 120)

FOR *the* FILLING

2 large sweet potatoes

½ cup (4 oz/125 g) mascarpone
cheese

1 large shallot, minced

Grated zest of ½ large lemon,
plus a bit of the juice

Pinch of red pepper flakes

Kosher salt

½ cup (4 oz/125 g) unsalted butter

2 oz (60 g) hot cacciatorini, cut into
julienne (about ½ cup)

Pinch of red pepper flakes

⅓ cup (3 oz/90 g) pure
maple syrup

½ cup (3 oz/90 g) finely chopped
pepperoncini, plus ¼ cup (2 fl oz/
60 ml) of the pickling liquid

Kosher salt

½ cup (½ oz/15 g) very roughly
chopped fresh flat-leaf parsley

Make the pasta dough as directed and let rest for 30 minutes.

To make the filling, bring a pot of water to a boil. Add the potatoes in their skins and cook until tender when pierced with a knife. Drain and let cool slightly. Peel off the skins and pass the potato flesh through a food mill into a large bowl. Add the mascarpone, shallot, lemon zest and juice, red pepper flakes, and salt to taste and mix until thoroughly combined. Scoop the filling into a piping bag fitted with a small tip or a resealable plastic bag with a corner snipped off.

To fill the pasta: First off, put some lightly salted water on for cooking the tortelli. Roll the dough through the second-to-narrowest setting on the pasta machine. Using a pasta cutter or the tip of a sharp chef's knife, cut the dough into 2½-inch (6-cm) squares. Place a dot of filling in the center of each square—a nice bite but not too big—it should take up about one-third of the center. Lightly dampen the edges of the dough and fold the opposite corners together to form a triangle. Press gently to seal the edges and around the filling pocket. Trim the edges to make them pretty and even. Place the tortelli on a lightly floured baking sheet as they are finished. You should have 4–6 tortelli per person.

to ASSEMBLE In a large sauté pan over high heat, melt the butter. When it begins to sizzle and brown, add the cacciatorini and red pepper flakes and fry to crisp up the sausages a bit. Add the maple syrup, half of the chopped pepperoncini, and the pepperoncini liquid. Add a couple splashes of the pasta cooking water and a pinch of salt. Reduce the heat to medium and let the sauce simmer while you cook the tortelli.

Add the tortelli to the gently simmering water and cook just until they float to the top, about 3 minutes. Using a slotted spoon, transfer them to the butter sauce. Continue to cook until the sauce is reduced enough to cling nicely to the pasta.

To serve, divide the tortelli among pasta bowls or plates. Drizzle a bit of the sauce and meat from the pan on top. Garnish with the remaining peppers and the parsley and serve right away.

HOW WE MAKE
RISOTTO

Risotto is on the opposite end of the cooking spectrum from the set-it-and-forget-it recipe family. It requires attention and nurturing. It is a famed Italian rice dish, of course, but it is also a cooking method that can be applied to any grain or even to dried pasta. The process calls for slowly adding liquid to the raw rice to achieve a creamy texture. Risotto can be stressful, though it doesn't need to be. We find that parcooking the rice makes the whole process a lot easier for two reasons: you can prep the dish up to 2 days in advance, and on the day of serving, much less stirring and slaving at the stove is required, giving you more time to hang out with your guests.

Risotto should be creamy but not gummy—and certainly never mushy. It is rice, and although it has put on this amazing creamy costume, you should still be able to tell that it is rice. In other words, it must retain an al dente bite. The most popular types of risotto rice are Arborio, Carnaroli, and Vialone Nano, all members of a starchy short-grain family. At Sorella, Carnaroli is our favorite. It has good flavor and handles the parcooking step especially well. Save the Vialone Nano for when you are a risotto pro, as it is the most delicate and thus the easiest to screw up.

BASIC PAR COOKED RISOTTO

MAKES ABOUT 4 CUPS (20 OZ)

2 qt (2 l) warm water
or chicken stock

½ cup (4 fl oz/125 ml)
extra-virgin olive oil

2 large shallots, minced

2 cups (14 oz/440 g)
Carnaroli rice

2 cups (16 fl oz/500 ml)
dry white wine

Kosher salt

Pour the water or stock into a pot and bring almost to a boil over high heat. Reduce to low and keep warm.

In a rondeau or deep, heavy sauté pan, warm the olive oil over medium heat. Add the shallots and sweat until translucent, about 3 minutes. You do not want color on the shallots. Add the rice and cook, stirring often, until it is glossy, 2–3 minutes. (This is called "parching" the rice; you are opening up the pores on the grains so they can more easily absorb liquid.)

Stir in the wine, bring to a simmer, and cook until reduced by half. At this point, start to add liquid slowly and stir with loving care. Using a ladle, add about 1 cup (8 fl oz/250 ml) of the water or stock, simmer, stirring constantly so the rice does not scorch. When the liquid has been absorbed, add another ladleful. Continue to simmer and stir. Repeat a few more times, waiting until the liquid is absorbed after each addition before adding more.

To know when the rice is done, bite it. Pick out a grain and bite it in half between your two front teeth. If it slips out and does not break, add more liquid a little at a time and keep cooking. If you can bite it in half, then look at the inside of the grain and see how big the pure white raw speck in the middle is. When we par cook risotto at Sorella, we take our rice to about 85 percent cooked through. The white part at the center of the grain should take up about one-third of the space. You may not need all of the liquid to reach this point.

When the risotto is ready, pour it onto a baking sheet to cool. When cooled completely, transfer it to an airtight container. The cooked risotto will keep in the refrigerator for up to 3 days.

You now have the base for whatever risotto you feel like making. Because of the amount of tasting and care that goes into risotto, it's one of those dishes that we change often so we can taste something new. Three of our seasonal favorites follow. But armed with this basic recipe, you can invent your own great risotto.

SPICY
SHRIMP RISOTTO

SERVES 4–8

This colorful risotto is a play on Cioppino, a San Francisco classic, but features shrimp instead of crab. The sourdough crunch adds a nice textural element and emphasizes the tie-in to the Bay Area. It's a rich, stewy, savory dish that is delicious any time of year. Our risottos serve four as a main course or eight as a first course.

FOR *the* SHRIMP STOCK

¼ cup (2 fl oz/60 ml) extra-virgin olive oil

Shells and heads from shrimp (below), chopped

2 large shallots, chopped

4 cloves garlic, chopped

1 or 2 habanero chiles, chopped

¾ cup (6 oz/185 g) tomato paste

2 cups (10 oz/315 g) drained canned plum tomatoes, preferably San Marzano, chopped

4 cups (32 fl oz/1 l) dry red wine

Pinch of sugar

A few bay leaves

½ cup (4 oz/125 g) unsalted butter, at room temperature

1 yellow onion, minced

2 red bell peppers, seeded and minced

3 cloves garlic, minced

Grated zest of 1 orange

1 cup (5 oz/155 g) drained canned plum tomatoes, preferably San Marzano, chopped

1 batch Par Cooked Risotto (page 135)

4 or 5 Ruby Red shrimp (from the Gulf Coast) or other high-quality shrimp per person, peeled, deveined, and cut into 1-inch (2.5-cm) pieces

Kosher salt and freshly ground pepper

½ cup (½ oz/15 g) fresh flat-leaf parsley leaves, chopped

1 cup (2 oz/60 g) fresh sourdough bread crumbs, toasted in butter until golden

To make the shrimp stock, in a stockpot over high heat, warm the olive oil. Add the shrimp shells and heads and cook until their color brightens, smashing them up as you stir. Add the shallots, garlic, and chile(s) and cook for a moment, until fragrant. Add the tomato paste, stir well, and cook until rust colored. Add the tomatoes, wine, sugar, and bay leaves. Add water if needed to cover the shells with liquid. Bring to a boil, then reduce the heat to medium and simmer until the stock is rich in flavor and color, about 1 hour. Remove from the heat, strain through a sieve lined with cheesecloth, and set aside.

In a frying pan, melt half of the butter over medium heat. Add the onion, bell peppers, and garlic and sweat until the onion is translucent, about 8 minutes. Add the orange zest and tomatoes and cook until the liquid the tomatoes release reduces slightly. Remove from the heat and set aside.

to ASSEMBLE In a large saucepan or large, deep sauté pan, combine the rice, the onion mixture, and about 2 cups (16 fl oz/500 ml) of the stock and stir to mix well. Place over medium heat and cook until the rice is almost tender, tasting for doneness. Add the shrimp and the remaining butter and continue to stir while the butter melts and the sauce emulsifies. Cook until the rice is creamy and tender. Add another splash of the stock if needed. Taste and adjust the seasoning with salt and pepper. Stir in the parsley. Spoon the risotto onto plates or into bowls. Garnish with the bread crumbs for some crunch and serve right away.

BRAISED OXTAIL
RISOTTO

SERVES 4–8

After Italy, Emma started cooking like crazy in our apartment. She made this risotto for an Italian friend. He couldn't believe that a twenty-one-year-old non-Italian woman had cooked the best risotto he had ever tasted. The recipe landed on the menu our first winter.

FOR *the* BRAISED OXTAIL

½ cup (4 fl oz/125 ml) extra-virgin olive oil

6–8 lb (3–4 kg) oxtails

Kosher salt

All-purpose flour for dusting

3 or 4 carrots, peeled and chopped

2 yellow onions, chopped

4 ribs celery, chopped

6 cloves garlic, chopped

2 oranges, chopped (with the peel)

½ cup (4 oz/125 g) tomato paste

2 cups (16 fl oz/500 ml) dry white wine

2 cups (16 fl oz/500 ml) apple juice

A few *each* fresh thyme sprigs, bay leaves, whole cloves, whole allspice, and black peppercorns

Extra-virgin olive oil and butter for pan

1 yellow onion, thinly sliced

Kosher salt

1 batch Par Cooked Risotto (page 135)

1 cup (6 oz/185 g) pitted prunes, finely chopped

3 Tbsp fresh thyme leaves, chopped

Grated zest of 1 large orange

6–8 oz (185–250 g) Robiola Bosina cheese or a mild brie, cut into small cubes

½ cup (4 oz/125 g) unsalted butter, cut into small cubes

Grated young pecorino cheese for serving

Fresh flat-leaf parsley leaves, torn, for garnish

Preheat the oven to 225°F (110°C).

To make the braised oxtail, pour the olive oil into a roasting pan on the stove top (you may need to use 2 burners) and heat over high heat. Dry off the oxtails and season them liberally with salt. Give them a dust with some flour and place in the hot oil to sear, turning with tongs as needed to brown on all sides. When they are deeply brown all over, transfer to a plate and set aside.

Pour off some of the excess fat from the pan and throw in the carrots, onions, celery, garlic, and oranges. Reduce the heat to medium and sauté until the vegetables are nicely browned and slightly caramelized, 8–10 minutes, being careful not to burn. Add the tomato paste, stir well, and cook until rust colored. Add the wine and apple juice and deglaze the pan, stirring to scrape up any browned bits from the pan bottom.

Return the oxtails to the pan and add the thyme, bay leaves, cloves, allspice, and peppercorns. Add water if needed just to cover the oxtails. Cover the pan tightly with aluminum foil, transfer to the oven, and braise until the meat is falling off the bones, about 3 hours. Remove from the oven and let cool in the braising liquid to room temperature, then refrigerate overnight. (If you are short on time, skip this step.)

In a small pan over medium heat, warm a drizzle of olive oil and a dab of butter. Add the onion and sprinkle with a bit of salt to draw out the moisture. Cook, stirring from time to time and being careful not to let the onion burn, until it is soft and caramel colored, about 10 minutes. Remove from the heat and set aside.

Return the roasting pan to a low oven to warm so you can remove the oxtail meat. When warm, pull the meat from the bones. Break up the big chunks with your hands and set aside. Put the bones in a saucepan, add the braising liquid, including the vegetables, and bring to a simmer over medium heat. Cook until the sauce is reduced enough to coat the back of a spoon, about 30 minutes. Strain through a fine-mesh sieve into a bowl. Taste and season with salt. Set aside.

to ASSEMBLE In a large saucepan or deep, heavy sauté pan, combine the rice, oxtail meat, caramelized onion, prunes, thyme, and some of the orange zest. Place over medium heat and add about a ladleful of the sauce. Bring to a simmer and cook, stirring constantly, until the rice is tender all the way through, about 8 minutes.

When the rice takes on a creamy character, start dropping in bits of the Robiola cheese and butter and continue to stir. Then taste and assess. Is it creamy enough? Does it need more liquid? Is it too thick? Does it need salt? Is it too runny? Does it need acid? It should be creamy and savory with a touch of sweetness from the prunes and onions. The orange zest should bring out the meat and braising liquid; add more if necessary.

When the risotto is ultra sexy looking, serve right away, spooning it onto plates or into bowls. Garnish with the pecorino and parsley.

RISOTTO

with

PORCINI
RAGÙ

We created this dish for a wine dinner with Alberto Longo, one of our favorite winemakers. Porcini and bacon are often served together with pasta in Longo's hometown in Puglia, where most of the land is dedicated to growing vegetables and grains. For the dinner, we tossed this *ragù* with *orecchiette*. From there, it evolved into this very tasty risotto.

FOR *the* PORCINI RAGÙ

¼ cup (2 fl oz/60 ml) extra-virgin olive oil

8 oz (250 g) guanciale, cut into small dice (about 2 cups)

4 or 5 shallots, minced

6–8 cloves garlic, sliced

4 cups (4 oz/125 g) dried porcini mushrooms, reconstituted and chopped, liquid reserved

½ cup (½ oz/15 g) minced fresh sage

2 Tbsp fresh thyme leaves, minced

Grated zest of 1 orange

Grated zest of 1 lemon

2 cups (16 fl oz/500 ml) dry white wine

3 cups (24 fl oz/750 ml) whole milk

1 cup (8 fl oz/250 ml) heavy cream

Kosher salt and freshly ground pepper

A few bay leaves

1 batch Par Cooked Risotto (page 135)

½ cup (¾ oz/20 g) roughly chopped fresh sage

½ lemon

½ cup (4 oz/125 g) unsalted butter, at room temperature, cut into small cubes

2 oz (60 g) young pecorino cheese, grated (about ½ cup)

Fresh flat-leaf parsley leaves for garnish

To make the ragù, in a large saucepan over medium heat, warm the olive oil. Add the guanciale and fry until the fat is rendered and the pork is translucent, 5–8 minutes. Add the shallots and garlic and cook until the shallots are softened, another minute or two. Add the porcini, give the mixture a few stirs, and add the minced sage, the thyme, and the citrus zests to the pan. Pour in the white wine, bring to a simmer, and cook to reduce a bit.

Add the milk, cream, a hefty dose of salt, a few grinds of pepper, and the bay leaves. Stir again to combine. Cover, reduce the heat to low, and cook, stirring every 15 minutes or so, until the ragù cooks down to a stewlike consistency, at least 1 hour and up to 2½ hours. Give it a taste to make sure the flavors have mellowed and any alcohol taste from the wine has cooked away. Taste and adjust the seasoning with salt and pepper. Remove from the heat. Cover to keep warm and set aside.

In a large saucepan or deep, heavy sauté pan, combine the rice with about two-thirds of the porcini ragù if cooking for 4–6 and all of it if cooking for 6–8. Thin the ragù with a bit of water if necessary. (Store leftover ragù in an airtight container in the fridge for up to 4 days.) Place over medium heat, bring to a simmer, and cook, stirring constantly, until the rice is tender all the way through and takes on a creamy character, about 8 minutes. Add the chopped sage and a squeeze of lemon juice, stir to incorporate, then stir in the butter. Remove from the heat and stir in a hefty handful of the pecorino, reserving some for garnish.

To serve, spoon the risotto onto plates or into bowls. Sprinkle with the remaining pecorino and the parsley and serve right away.

STASERA ABBIAMO

Braised Oxtail with Creamy Polenta, Fried Eggs, and Garlic Toast 144

Veal Stew with Herb Dumplings 147

Hanger Steak with Garlic-Herb Butter, Castelvetrano Olives,
and Charred Green Onions 148

Lamb Chops with Curried Autumn Vegetables and Feta Vinaigrette 151

Stuffed Meatballs with Caramelized Onions and Arugula 152

Cider-Brined Pork Chops with Smoked Cherry Tomato Vinaigrette,
Olive Mashed Potatoes, and Garlic Chips 158

Crispy Duck Leg Confit with Fregola Sarda,
Plum-Shallot Agrodolce, and Greek Yogurt 161

Grilled Quail with Crispy Potatoes, Prosciutto Cotto, Aioli, and Beet Butter 162

Roasted Guinea Hens with Creamed Corn, Escarole, and Hot Chile Jam 165

Scallops with Parsnip Purée, Candied Grapefruit, and Crispy Prosciutto 166

Butter-Poached Langoustine with Lobster Glace,
Purple Pearl Barley, Spring Peas, and Dill 169

Poached Hawaiian Blue Prawns with Creamy Polenta,
Old Bay Croutons, and Calabrian Chiles 170

Arctic Char with Tomato-Braised Romano Beans and Mustard-Glazed Bacon 172

Golden Tilefish with Shiitake Crema, Crispy Mushrooms,
and Glazed Spring Vegetables 173

Pan-Seared Mackerel with Vidalia–Pine Nut Purée, Pickles, and Apricots 175

In Bologna, we ate at a tiny, hidden-away restaurant unlike any place
we had ever experienced. It was so dark that we could barely see each
other. Our waiter, an adorable old man with a moustache, greeted us
warmly in Italian but did not give us menus. We let him know that we
didn't speak Italian very well, and he said, "My English is not so good,
but tonight we have…" He went on to name a few dishes and then
walked away. "I can't wait to see a menu. The specials sound amazing,"
Emma said. We soon realized that what our waiter had recited were
not the specials. It turned out the restaurant had only a verbal menu,
and our sweet waiter had named all of the dishes offered.
We, of course, ordered everything.

Stasera abbiamo translates to "tonight we have," and this chapter
is meant to channel the kind of dining experience we had that
night in Bologna. At Sorella, we wanted to create that same sense
of warmth, of being tucked away at a table in someone's home.
We change this menu often. Because our fellow Americans are more
comfortable with an appetizer and main course scenario, these
are like main dishes—a selection of our favorite specials.

BRAISED
OXTAIL
with
CREAMY POLENTA,
FRIED EGGS, *and* GARLIC TOAST

SERVES 4–6

This dish is warming and decadent and perfect for brunch, lunch, or dinner. You'll need to start the oxtail component a day in advance, but you'll be rewarded for that effort. Trust us. In fact, this dish is so good that we stir the same braised oxtail, with just a minor change, into risotto on page 138.

Braised Oxtail (page 138), substituting 2 cups (16 fl oz/ 500 ml) whole milk for the apple juice

Kosher salt and freshly ground pepper

1 Tbsp unsalted butter

1 batch Creamy Polenta (page 185)

8–12 slices good-quality ciabatta, or baguette (cut on the diagonal into crostini about 6 inches/15 cm long)

Extra-virgin olive oil for brushing

2 cloves garlic, cut in half lengthwise

4–6 eggs

Freshly grated Parmesan cheese for garnish

Prepare the oxtail as directed, adding the milk in place of the apple juice. Reduce the braising liquid as directed and strain through a fine-mesh sieve placed over a saucepan. Taste and season with salt and pepper. Place over medium heat, add the oxtail meat, and warm gently. Stir in the butter, then taste and adjust the seasoning.

to ASSEMBLE Gently rewarm the polenta, if necessary. Brush the bread slices with olive oil and toast them in a toaster or under the broiler until golden. While they are still warm, vigorously rub with the garlic clove halves and sprinkle with a bit of salt.

In a frying pan, fry the eggs sunny-side up and season with salt and pepper.

Spoon the polenta into individual shallow bowls or onto plates and top with a big scoop of the braised oxtail. Place an egg on top of each serving. Put 2 crostini on each plate and garnish the plate with a shower of Parmesan. Serve right away.

VEAL STEW

with

HERB DUMPLINGS

SERVES 4–6

The dumplings in this luxurious stew are similar to spaetzle.
Flavor them with any herb (or herb mixture) you like.
They are delicious with braised meat, as in this dish,
or served on their own with butter and cheese.

2 lb (1 kg) veal stew meat, cut into 1½-inch (4-cm) cubes

¼ cup (2 fl oz/60 ml) extra-virgin olive oil

Kosher salt and freshly ground pepper

4 carrots, peeled and cut into bite-size pieces

2 yellow onions, diced

3 ribs celery, diced

5 large cloves garlic, thinly sliced

1½ cup (4 oz/125 g) tomato paste

1½ cups (12 fl oz/375 ml) dry white wine

½ cup (4 fl oz/125 ml) whole milk

Pinch of grated orange zest

Pinch of grated lemon zest

¼ cup (¼ oz/7 g) packed fresh marjoram leaves, roughly chopped

2 Tbsp fresh thyme leaves, roughly chopped

5 bay leaves

FOR *the* DUMPLINGS

2 cups (10 oz/315 g) all-purpose flour

1 Tbsp kosher salt

1¼ cups (10 fl oz/310 ml) whole milk

5 large eggs, beaten

⅓ cup (1½ oz/45 g) grated Parmesan cheese

⅓ cup (⅓ oz/10 g) chopped fresh herbs

4 Tbsp (2 oz/60 g) unsalted butter, plus 3 Tbsp butter for finishing

Kosher salt and freshly ground pepper

Grated Parmesan cheese for serving

Chopped fresh flat-leaf parsley for garnish

Preheat the oven to 225°F (110°C).

Trim any silver skin off of the veal and pat dry. Heat the olive oil in a sauté pan over high heat until almost smoking. Just before you put the meat in the pan, season it liberally with salt. Brown off the cubes of veal, turning as needed, until they are golden brown on all sides, 6–8 minutes total.

Transfer the veal to a large Dutch oven or rondeau. Pour off all but about 2 Tbsp of fat from the sauté pan (do not wipe clean) and return to high heat. Add the carrots and sauté until softened and starting to caramelize, about 5 minutes. Add the onions and celery and sweat for a few minutes. Stir in the garlic and reduce the heat to medium. Make a space in the middle of the pan, spoon the tomato paste into the space, and cook until rust colored, about 5 minutes. Pour in the wine and deglaze the pan, stirring to scrape up any browned bits from the pan bottom. Add the contents of the sauté pan to the pot with the veal. Add the milk, citrus zests, marjoram, thyme, bay leaves, a good amount of salt, and a few grinds of pepper and give everything a stir. Add a bit of water if needed, so that the veal pieces are mostly covered. Cover the pot tightly and place in the oven. Roast until the meat is fork-tender, about 4 hours.

While the stew is cooking, make the dumplings: In a large bowl, whisk together the flour and salt. Add the milk and eggs and combine with your hands until a gooey batter forms. Start to shape and spank the dough in an upward motion in the bowl until a smooth, loose, and slightly elastic batter forms, about 12 minutes. Fold in the cheese and herbs. Cover the dough and let rest for 20 minutes or so.

Bring a saucepan of salted water to a boil over high heat. Set a large bowl of ice water nearby. Put a handful of the dumpling dough in a colander or spaetzle maker and press it through the holes with a rubber spatula into the boiling water. Boil until the dumplings float to the top, 2–3 minutes. Using a slotted spoon, transfer the dumplings to the ice bath. Repeat to cook the remaining dough. When all of the dumplings are cooked and cooled, scoop them out of the ice bath and set aside.

Remove the stew from the oven and let cool slightly. Meanwhile, in a sauté pan, melt the 4 Tbsp butter over medium heat. Add the dumplings to the melted butter along with a splash of water. Cook, stirring, until the water and butter have emulsified and reduced to a nice silky sauce, about 4 minutes. Taste for salt and add a grind or two of pepper. Toss in a bit of Parmesan as well.

to **ASSEMBLE** Spoon off any excess fat or foam from the top of the stew. Taste and adjust the seasoning. Stir in the 3 Tbsp butter. Put a heaping scoop of the dumplings in individual shallow soup bowls or onto dinner plates, followed by a large spoonful of the veal stew. Garnish with the cheese and parsley and serve right away.

HANGER STEAK

with

GARLIC-HERB BUTTER, CASTELVETRANO OLIVES, *and* CHARRED GREEN ONIONS

SERVES 4–6

This dish is the perfect example of how we like our food at Sorella: simple, clean, and tasty. It's straightforward enough to eat on a weekday night but can also be jazzed up for a special dinner. The steak is the star of this dish, so using a good piece of meat can make all the difference. The buttery and mild Castelvetrano olives, native to Sicily, are wonderful in pastas with braised meats, salads, and dressings, or on their own as a snack.

FOR *the* GARLIC-HERB BUTTER

1 plump head garlic, minced

1 cup (1 oz/30 g) packed fresh basil leaves, finely chopped

½ cup (¾ oz/20 g) minced fresh chives

½ cup (½ oz/15 g) packed fresh flat-leaf parsley leaves, finely chopped

Grated zest of 2 lemons

1 Tbsp kosher salt

1 lb (500 g) unsalted butter, at room temperature

4–6 hanger steaks, about ½ lb (250 g) each

Kosher salt

Extra-virgin olive oil for charring

2 bunches green onions

1 cup (6 oz/185 g) Castelvetrano olives, pitted and chopped

1 lemon, halved (optional)

To make the garlic-herb butter, in a large frying pan over low heat, combine the garlic, basil, chives, parsley, lemon zest, salt, and butter. Melt the butter, stirring the ingredients together to mix well. Remove from the heat and let sit for a couple of hours. Don't skimp on time; the butter is more flavorful if allowed to sit for awhile.

Pat the steaks dry. In a large frying pan, pour in enough olive oil to cover the pan bottom and place over high heat. You want enough oil to get into all of the nooks and crannies of the meat, but not as much as you would use if you were panfrying. Just before you are ready to add the steaks to the hot oil, season them generously with salt, pressing the granules into the meat. Cook, turning once, until you get a nice dark char all around the steaks, about 2 minutes per side for medium-rare. (Be careful not to crowd the steaks in the pan or you will steam the meat. If necessary, use 2 pans or work in batches.)

Transfer the steaks to the pan with the melted garlic-herb butter and let rest for about 15 minutes.

To char the green onions, warm a drizzle of olive oil in a stove-top grill pan over medium heat. Add the green onions to the pan and cook, turning as needed, until nicely charred on all sides, 6–8 minutes. Transfer to a cutting board and chop.

to ASSEMBLE Lift the steaks from the butter, letting the excess fall back into the pan, and transfer to a cutting board. Carve across the grain into thin slices. Divide the slices among dinner plates. Drizzle with some of the flavored butter and scatter the olives and green onions on top. Finish with a squeeze of lemon juice, if you like. Serve right away.

LAMB CHOPS

with

CURRIED AUTUMN VEGETABLES *and* FETA VINAIGRETTE

SERVES 4–6

The feta vinaigrette, a natural with lamb, is versatile and can be used on salads or other roasted meats. Marjoram is one of our favorite herbs. It smells ultra feminine and exotic. Rub any leftover leaves on your wrists when you're done cooking.

FOR *the* VINAIGRETTE

½ cup (4 fl oz/125 ml) extra-virgin olive oil

¼ lb (125 g) feta cheese, preferably goat's milk, crumbled

2 Tbsp chopped fresh marjoram

1 tsp grated lemon zest

1 tsp freshly ground pepper

Pinch of kosher salt

FOR *the* CURRIED VEGETABLES

6 Tbsp (3 oz/90 g) unsalted butter

3 carrots, peeled and cut into 2-inch (5-cm) pieces

2 parsnips, peeled and cut into 1-inch (2.5-cm) pieces

1 large turnip, peeled and cut into 1-inch (2.5-cm) pieces

3 cloves garlic, sliced

1 shallot, roughly chopped

⅓ cup (4 oz/125 g) honey

⅓ cup (3 fl oz/80 ml) sherry vinegar

2 Tbsp curry powder

2 Tbsp kosher salt

⅓ cup (2 oz/60 g) dried currants

4 lamb rib chops or 2 nice-size lamb loin chops per person

Kosher salt and freshly ground pepper

3 Tbsp unsalted butter

3 Tbsp extra-virgin olive oil

Chopped fresh marjoram for garnish

To make the vinaigrette, in a bowl, whisk together the olive oil, feta, marjoram, lemon zest, pepper, and salt until well combined but still chunky. Set aside at room temperature.

Preheat the oven to 300°F (150°C).

To make the vegetables, in a small flameproof roasting pan on the stove top, melt the butter over medium heat. Add the carrots, parsnips, turnip, garlic, and shallot and toss to distribute evenly. Add the honey, vinegar, ¼ cup (2 fl oz/60 ml) water, the curry powder, and the salt and stir to mix and coat well. Fold in the currants. Cover the pan with aluminum foil and transfer to the oven. Roast until the vegetables are just tender, about 20 minutes. Take off the foil and raise the oven temperature to 400°F (200°C). Continue roasting, stirring occasionally, until fully tender and caramelized a bit, about 5 minutes longer. Remove from the oven. Re-cover with the foil to keep warm. Set aside. Leave the oven on.

Trim any silver skin off of the lamb chops. Pat the chops dry and season them with salt and pepper.

In a large ovenproof sauté pan or roasting pan over high heat, melt the butter in the olive oil. Place the chops in the pan, fat side down (the edge of the chops), and brown on the first edge, about 2 minutes. Turn to a flat side and brown for 2 minutes. Continue until browned on all sides. Transfer to the oven and roast for about 10 more minutes for medium-rare, depending on the size of the chops. Remove from the oven and let rest for 5–10 minutes. Slice into individual chops between the bones.

to ASSEMBLE Mound a portion of the vegetables on each dinner plate. Arrange the lamb chops on top. Top each chop with a hefty spoonful of the vinaigrette, garnish with a sprinkle of marjoram, and serve right away.

STUFFED
MEATBALLS
with
CARAMELIZED ONIONS
and ARUGULA

SERVES 6

FOR *the* MEATBALLS

½ lb (250 g) ground beef

½ lb (250 g) ground veal

1 lb (500 g) ground pork

4 Tbsp extra-virgin olive oil

6 shallots, minced

1½ large heads garlic, minced

1 cup (1 oz/30 g) packed fresh
basil leaves, chopped

1 cup (1 oz/30 g) packed fresh
flat-leaf parsley leaves, chopped

1 tsp freshly grated nutmeg

Grated zest and juice of 1 large orange

Grated zest of 1 large lemon

1 cup (8 fl oz/250 ml)
heavy cream

1½ cups (6 oz/185 g)
dried bread crumbs

¼ lb (125 g) Parmesan cheese,
grated (about 1 cup)

2 large eggs, beaten

2½ Tbsp kosher salt

Freshly ground pepper

Six 2-inch (5-cm) cubes smoked
mozzarella cheese

Vegetable oil for frying

Veal demi-glace, homemade
(page 233) or purchased, as needed

Ingredients continued

This dish was created for *Iron Chef* and led to a lot of ball jokes from Alton Brown. *Tonnato* is a creamy tuna sauce that is most commonly served cold with veal. We also like to dip *grissini* in it. The sauce first appeared in Piemontese cookbooks in the nineteenth century, when items such as tuna, anchovies, capers, and olives were regularly arriving in the province from Liguria.

To make the meatballs, put the beef, veal, and pork in a large bowl and crumble it with your hands to combine. Set aside.

In a small sauté pan over medium heat, warm the olive oil. Add the shallots and garlic and sweat until translucent, about 3 minutes. Add the basil, parsley, and nutmeg and sauté until the herbs are fragrant, a minute or two. Remove from the heat and let the mixture cool slightly, then add it to the meat mixture. Add the orange and lemon zests and the orange juice to the bowl and start to combine, still using your hands. Add the cream, bread crumbs, Parmesan, eggs, salt, and pepper and mix just until you have a cohesive mass. Do not overmix.

Make a tiny test patty. Wipe clean the pan in which you sautéed the shallots and garlic and drizzle in a little olive oil. Cook off your test patty. Try it and see if the seasoning needs adjusting. Once you are happy with the taste, roll the meatballs: Take up a 5–6 oz (155–185 g) portion of the meat mixture (about the size of a big fist) and shape it around a cube of mozzarella into a ball. Repeat with the remaining meat mixture and mozzarella cubes.

Preheat the oven to 250°F (120°C).

To brown off the meatballs, pour vegetable oil into a sauté pan with tall sides or a deep fryer to a depth of 3 inches (7.5 cm) and heat to 360°F (185°C). Working in batches if necessary to avoid crowding the pan (you don't want the meatballs to steam), add the meatballs and brown, turning as necessary, until richly colored on all sides. Drain off the excess oil, then transfer the meatballs to a roasting pan and pour in the demi-glace to come about one-third of the way up the sides of the balls. Cover and braise for 25–30 minutes.

Recipe method continued

FOR *the* CARAMELIZED ONIONS

½ cup (4 oz/125 g) unsalted butter

4 yellow onions, cut into julienne

Kosher salt and freshly ground pepper

1 cup (8 fl oz/250 ml) veal demi-glace

1 cup (8 fl oz/250 ml) brandy

FOR *the* TONNATO SAUCE

¼ cup (2 fl oz/60 ml) veal demi-glace

2 large egg yolks

4 anchovy fillets, mashed

2 Tbsp capers, mashed

Grated zest and juice of 1 lemon

1 tsp red wine vinegar

Kosher salt

½ cup (4 fl oz/125 ml) extra-virgin olive oil

1 can (6 oz/185 g) high-quality olive oil–packed tuna, drained

Pinch of sugar (optional)

¼ lb (125 g) smoked mozzarella, grated (about 1 cup)

A few handfuls of arugula leaves

Meanwhile, make the caramelized onions: In a sauté pan over medium heat, melt the butter. Add the onions, stir to coat, and reduce the heat to medium-low. Low and slow is the game here: you want to coax all the sugars out of the onions. Add a big pinch of salt and a grind or two of pepper. Cook, stirring occasionally, until the onions are a uniform dark gold, about 20 minutes. Add the demi-glace and the brandy and simmer until nicely thickened—not quite dry but not soupy, either. Taste to make sure the alcohol taste has burned off, and adjust the seasoning. Set aside and cover to keep warm.

To make the tonnato sauce, in a bowl, whisk together the demi-glace, the egg yolks, anchovies, capers, lemon zest and juice, vinegar, and a hefty pinch of salt. Whisking vigorously, slowly stream in the olive oil. Add the tuna and continue to beat until smooth and airy. (You can also make the sauce in a food processor or blender.) The sauce should have the consistency of mayonnaise. Give it a taste and see if it needs more salt or acid, or that pinch of sugar. Set aside.

to ASSEMBLE Remove the meatballs from the oven. Raise the oven temperature to 400°F (200°C). Take the meatballs out of the demi-glace and place on a baking sheet. Top each ball with a sprinkle of the mozzarella. Place in the oven just to melt the cheese. Spoon some tonnato sauce on the bottom half of each dinner plate and place a spoonful of caramelized onions in the center of the plate. Rest a meatball on top of each portion of onions and garnish with the arugula leaves. Serve right away.

As restaurateurs, we thrive on controlled chaos. The feeling at the end of a crazy night is a natural high unlike any other. We are masters of the illusion that all this is easy, when in fact it's hard as hell. The end of the night, sitting together over a glass of wine and silently communicating about the night, is the best.

CIDER-BRINED
PORK CHOPS
with

SMOKED CHERRY TOMATO VINAIGRETTE, OLIVE MASHED POTATOES, *and* GARLIC CHIPS

SERVES 4–6

A few years ago, Emma went through a phase of hot and cold smoking anything she could get her hands on. Some ingredients took on too much smoke, some not enough, but the sweet heirloom tomatoes of late summer were a triumph. The combination of sweet and smoky creates an unexpected bacony flavor before you even introduce the pork. Plan on brining the chops overnight for the most flavorful result.

FOR *the* CIDER-BRINED PORK CHOPS

4 cups (32 fl oz/1 l) apple cider

½ cup (4 fl oz/125 ml) cider vinegar

1 cup (8 oz/250 g) kosher salt, plus extra for sprinkling

1 cup (8 oz/250 g) sugar

4–6 bone-in center-cut pork chops

Olive oil for rubbing and drizzling

FOR *the* SMOKED CHERRY TOMATO VINAIGRETTE

About 40 cherry tomatoes

2 handfuls apple-wood chips

½ cup (4 fl oz/125 ml) extra-virgin olive oil

2 Tbsp red wine vinegar

Pinch of sugar

Kosher salt and freshly ground pepper

FOR *the* OLIVE MASHED POTATOES

1½ lb (750 g) fingerling potatoes, scrubbed but not peeled

1 cup (6 oz/185 g) drained jarred oil-packed Taggiasca or other dark, buttery olives, pitted, oil reserved

Pinch of grated orange zest

¼ tsp lemon juice

Kosher salt and freshly ground pepper

To brine the pork chops, in a large pot, combine the cider, cider vinegar, salt, sugar, and 3 qt (3 l) water. Bring to a simmer over medium-high heat, stirring to dissolve the salt and sugar, then remove from the heat and let cool to room temperature. Add the pork chops to the brine. Make sure the chops are completely submerged by placing a plate on top. Cover and refrigerate for at least 12 or up to 24 hours.

To make the vinaigrette, bring a small saucepan of water to a boil. Set a bowl of ice and water nearby. Make an X in the bottom of each tomato with a paring knife. Blanch the tomatoes for 20 seconds in the boiling water, then transfer to the ice bath to stop the cooking. Peel the tomatoes and put them in a heatproof colander. Place the colander in the upper third of a cold oven. Have 2 same-size sauté pans ready. Put the wood chips in one pan and light them. When the flame has grown, turn the second pan upside down and place it over the first pan to smother the flames. After the flames go out, slide the whole setup into the lower third of the oven, below the tomatoes. Slide the top pan off a bit to allow smoke to billow up to the tomatoes. Leave the tomatoes in there smoking for about 10 minutes. Transfer the tomatoes to a bowl and add the olive oil, vinegar, sugar, and salt and pepper to taste. Let sit at room temperature until ready to serve.

To make the olive mashed potatoes, bring a saucepan of water to a boil. Add the potatoes and boil until fork-tender, about 25 minutes. Meanwhile, on a cutting board, using the flat side of a chef's knife, or in a mortar using a pestle, smash the olives almost to a paste. Drain the potatoes well and transfer to a bowl. Add the olives, orange zest, and lemon juice and smash the potatoes while drizzling in ⅓ cup (3 fl oz/80 ml) of the oil from the olive jar (or use extra-virgin olive oil). Taste and season with salt and pepper.

Build a medium-hot fire in a charcoal grill. Scrape the rack clean and brush lightly with oil. While the grill is heating, in a small frying pan pour vegetable oil to a depth of about ¼ inch (6 mm) and place over medium heat until warm but definitely not smoking. (You want the moisture to release and the garlic chips to crisp, which takes a bit of time. If the oil is too hot, the garlic will burn before it has a chance to get crispy.) Sprinkle in the garlic slices and fry until light golden brown, about 4 minutes. Be careful not to let them burn, or they will be bitter. Transfer to paper towels to drain then sprinkle with a bit of salt. Let the oil get hot again, then toss in the basil leaves and fry until the leaves are silent in the oil after the initial sizzle, about 45 seconds. Transfer to the paper towels and sprinkle with salt.

Vegetable oil for frying

1 large head garlic, thinly sliced lengthwise with a mandoline or a sharp chef's knife

12 large fresh basil leaves

Remove the chops from the brine and pat dry. Rub with a little olive oil and sprinkle with a bit of salt. Arrange on the grill directly over the fire and grill for 5–7 minutes per side for medium-rare. Turn the chops only once so they get nice grill marks. Transfer to a cutting board, tent with aluminum foil, and let rest.

to ASSEMBLE Gently rewarm the potatoes. Put a scoop of the potatoes in the middle of each dinner plate and flatten slightly. Place a chop on top, followed by a spoonful of the tomato vinaigrette. Garnish with a sprinkle of the garlic chips and a couple of fried basil leaves. Drizzle with olive oil and grind pepper on top. Serve right away.

CRISPY
DUCK LEG CONFIT

with

FREGOLA SARDA, PLUM-SHALLOT AGRODOLCE, *and* GREEK YOGURT

SERVES 4–6

We are firm believers that anything cooked in its own fat will end up rocking (see Pork Rillette, page 57). If you have any extra duck, shred it and add to eggs the next morning or to pasta. Rendered duck fat can be found at specialty markets, online, and some butcher shops; D'Artagnan makes a good one. It works well for cooking anything that needs a serious sear and frying because of its high smoke point, plus it adds a luscious richness. At Sorella, we smear it on our English muffin bread before grilling. *Fregola sarda,* a toasted semolina pasta, is like Italian couscous and great in salads and soups.

FOR *the* CONFIT

4–6 duck legs

Kosher salt

4 whole cloves

6 black peppercorns

4 whole allspice

A few bay leaves

6 cloves garlic, sliced

1 cup (8 fl oz/250 ml) brandy

Rendered duck fat, as needed

FOR *the* AGRODOLCE

6 Tbsp (3 oz/90 g) unsalted butter

6 shallots, thinly sliced

2 cups (8 oz/250 g) plums or cherries, pitted and quartered

½ cup (4 fl oz/125 ml) red wine vinegar

Juice of ½ orange

¼ cup (2 oz/60 g) sugar

1 bay leaf

Pinch of red pepper flakes

Kosher salt and freshly ground pepper

1½ cups dried fregola sarda

4 Tbsp (2 oz/60 g) unsalted butter, at room temperature

Grated zest and juice of 1 lemon

Whole-milk plain Greek yogurt for serving

Fresh flat-leaf parsley leaves for garnish

To make the confit, coat the duck legs in a good amount of salt. In a spice grinder or in a mortar using a pestle, grind the cloves, peppercorns, allspice, and bay leaves coarsely. Press the mixture, along with the garlic, onto the legs. Put the legs in a pan with the brandy and turn to coat. Cover and refrigerate for 48 hours.

Preheat the oven to 200°F (95°C).

Rinse the duck legs and pat dry. In a Dutch oven or ovenproof sauté pan just large enough to fit the legs without crowding, melt enough duck fat to cover the legs completely. Add the legs and tuck to submerge them in the fat. Bring to a simmer over medium-high heat, then place, uncovered, in the oven. Braise until the legs are completely tender and the fat is translucent, about 6 hours. Remove the confit from the oven and let cool to room temperature. Cover and refrigerate, making sure the legs are completely submerged in the fat.

To make the agrodolce, in a sauté pan over medium heat, melt the butter. Add the shallots and plums and sweat for a couple of minutes. Add the vinegar, orange juice, sugar, bay leaf, red pepper flakes, and salt and pepper to taste. Simmer until reduced by half and any harshness from the vinegar has gone away, about 12 minutes. The reduction should be sweet and tangy. Set aside at room temperature.

Bring a large pot of heavily salted water to a boil. Add the fregola and cook until al dente. Drain and set aside. While the fregola is cooking, warm the confit in a low oven.

Heat a large sauté pan over high heat. Slide the duck legs out of their fat and wipe off most of the excess. Add the legs to the hot pan and sear on all sides until crispy, turning as needed. Reduce the heat to low to heat the legs all the way through while you get ready to serve.

***to* ASSEMBLE** In another large sauté pan over medium heat, toss together the fregola, agrodolce, butter, lemon zest and juice, and a splash or two of water. Cook, stirring, until the sauce has reduced to a buttery glaze and coats the fregola. Taste and adjust the seasoning.

Make a swoosh of yogurt on each dinner plate. Pile the fregola mixture next to it, and place a golden duck leg on top. Garnish with the parsley leaves and serve right away.

STASERA ABBIAMO

GRILLED QUAIL

with

CRISPY POTATOES, PROSCIUTTO COTTO, AIOLI, *and* BEET BUTTER

SERVES 4–6

This is based on a rabbit dish served with olives, beets, and *prosciutto cotto* that we had in Bologna. We love little birds and wanted to try a similar preparation with quail. "Semiboneless" means all bones except the wing and leg bones have been removed, allowing for easier eating (helpful as quail are such tiny birds). Quail are often sold in packs of four and keep well frozen. They are also delicious pan-seared or deep-fried (try dipping them in the tempura-type batter found on page 75).

FOR *the* BEET BUTTER

1 large red beet, trimmed with 1 inch (2.5 cm) of the stem intact

1 cup (8 oz/250 g) unsalted butter, at room temperature

1 tsp sugar

1 tsp kosher salt

Grated zest of ½ lemon

Pinch of grated orange zest

3 lb (1.5 kg) fingerling potatoes

4–6 semiboneless quail

Salt

Vegetable oil for deep-frying

Extra-virgin olive oil for sautéing

¼ lb (125 g) prosciutto cotto or good-quality artisanal ham, cut into julienne (about 1 cup)

1 cup (6 oz/185 g) Taggiasca or other dark, buttery olives, pitted and chopped

1 cup (8 fl oz/250 ml) Orange-Cayenne Aioli (page 230)

To make the beet butter, boil or roast (at about 375°F/190°C) the beet until very tender, 30–60 minutes. The time will vary depending on how big the beet is and how fresh. Let cool slightly. Peel the beet by rubbing with paper towels. Rinse gently and cut into 2-inch (5-cm) chunks.

In a food processor, combine the beet and butter and process until a smooth paste forms. Add the sugar, salt, and zests and process to mix well. Scrape the compound butter onto a large sheet of parchment or waxed paper. Fold the edge of the paper over the butter, then roll it into a log. Twist the ends of the paper tightly and place in the freezer until firm, about 2 hours. (The frozen butter grates beautifully on a Microplane grater and can be frozen for up to 2 months; cut off slices as needed and let thaw at room temperature.)

Bring a large pot of heavily salted water to a boil. Add the potatoes and boil until just fork-tender, about 25 minutes. Drain, let cool slightly, and break into large chunks. Set aside.

Build a hot fire in a charcoal grill. Scrape the rack clean and brush lightly with oil. Pat the quail dry and season liberally with salt. Arrange the quail on the grill rack directly over the fire and grill, turning as needed, until cooked through, about 3 minutes per side. (The quail can also be cooked in a stove-top grill pan over medium heat.) Transfer to a cutting board and let rest for about 5 minutes.

Meanwhile, pour vegetable oil into a saucepan or deep-fryer to a depth of about 5 inches (13 cm) and heat over high heat to 360°F (185°C). Add the potato chunks in batches (so as not to crowd them in the pan, causing them to steam) and fry until golden brown and crispy, about 3 minutes. Using a slotted spoon, transfer to paper towels to drain.

In a large sauté pan over medium heat, warm just enough olive oil to cover the bottom. Add the prosciutto cotto and olives and sauté for about 5 minutes until the prosciutto cotto is crispy.

to **ASSEMBLE** Add the potatoes to the pan with the prosciutto cotto mixture and toss to mix. Season with salt. Arrange a pile of the potato mixture on each dinner plate. Drizzle a good amount of the aioli on top. Using a large chef's knife, cut the quail in half lengthwise, and rest 2 halves on each pile of potatoes. Grate the beet butter on top. (We like to use a Microplane grater so it looks like pink snow.) Serve right away.

SARAH'S *drink note* Lots of delicious flavors—earthy, sweet, smoky—are happening in this dish. Drink a lighter red, something with bright fruit. A Grignolino would be nice, but a Pinot Noir would be good as well.

ROASTED
GUINEA HENS

with

CREAMED CORN, ESCAROLE, *and* HOT CHILE JAM

SERVES 6

This is a go-nuts-at-the-farmers'-market-before-summer-is-over kind of dish. Heirloom chiles come into season in mid-September and are the perfect complement to late-summer corn. We like to grab an extra handful for pickling and making jam that will last through the winter. If possible, brine the hens overnight.

1 cup (8 oz/250 g) kosher salt, plus more for seasoning

1 cup (8 oz/250 g) sugar

6 cloves garlic

A few bay leaves

3 guinea hens, 2½ lb (1.25 kg) each

½ cup (4 oz/125 g) unsalted butter, at room temperature

FOR *the* CREAMED CORN

4 Tbsp (2 oz/60 g) unsalted butter

2 large shallots, minced

Kernels from 8–10 ears fresh corn, cobs reserved

Grated zest and juice of 1 large lime

½ cup (4 fl oz/125 ml) heavy cream

Pinch of sugar

Salt and freshly ground pepper

⅓ cup (½ oz/15 g) minced fresh chives

FOR *the* ESCAROLE

3 Tbsp extra-virgin olive oil

2 large shallots, chopped

1 head escarole, cored and cut into bite-size pieces

Grated zest and juice of ½ lemon

Kosher salt and freshly ground pepper

½ cup (4 oz/125 g) duck fat or extra-virgin olive oil

¼ cup (2½ oz/75 g) Hot Chile Jam (page 232)

Minced fresh chives for garnish

In a large pot, combine the 1 cup salt, the sugar, garlic, bay leaves, and 4 qt (4 l) water. Bring to a simmer over medium-high heat, stirring to dissolve the salt and sugar, then remove from the heat and let cool to room temperature. Add the guinea hens to the brine. Make sure the hens are completely submerged by placing a plate on top. Cover and let brine for at least 5 hours or refrigerate up to overnight.

Preheat the oven to 225°F (110°C). Fit a baking sheet with a rack. Drain the hens and pat them completely dry. Rub all over with the butter. Sprinkle with more salt and arrange them on the prepared rack. Roast until an instant-read thermometer inserted into the thickest part of a thigh away from the bone registers 140°F (60°C), about 1 hour. The juices will still be slightly pink. Remove from the oven and let the hens cool until they can be handled. Raise the oven temperature to 450°F (230°C).

Cut the birds in half along the backbone, then cut between the breast halves and the leg quarters to yield 4 serving pieces per bird. Set aside.

To make the creamed corn, in a large frying pan over medium heat, melt the butter. Add the shallots and sweat until translucent, about 5 minutes. Add the corn kernels. Using the back of a knife, scrape the cobs over the pan to release the milk. Stir to combine and coat, then sweat the corn until it begins to soften, about 3 minutes. Stir in the lime zest and juice. Add the cream, sugar, and salt and pepper to taste and mix well. Bring to a gentle simmer and cook until the liquid reduces to a thick and creamy sauce. Fold in the chives. Give it a taste and adjust the seasoning as necessary. Remove from the heat. Cover and set aside.

To make the escarole, in a sauté pan over medium-high heat, warm the olive oil. Add the shallots and sauté until caramelized to a light gold, about 5 minutes. Add the escarole, stir to coat with the oil, and cook until it begins to wilt. Hit it with a squeeze of lemon juice then sprinkle in the zest and season with salt and pepper. Toss and stir for a minute or two, then remove from the heat and set aside.

In a large ovenproof frying pan, melt the duck fat over high heat until smoking. Add the hen pieces, skin side down, and sear until the skin is dark golden brown and crispy, about 4 minutes. Transfer to the oven and roast until cooked through, about 10 minutes. The thigh juices should run clear.

to ASSEMBLE Gently rewarm the creamed corn over low heat, then spread a generous spoonful on each dinner plate. Mound the escarole in the center of the creamed corn, dividing it evenly. Rest 1 guinea breast half and 1 thigh and leg piece on top. Add a few dollops of the jam to the plate (it's intense, so not too much). Garnish with chives and serve right away.

SCALLOPS

with

PARSNIP PURÉE,

CANDIED GRAPEFRUIT,
and CRISPY PROSCIUTTO

SERVES 4–6

1 cup (8 fl oz/250 ml)
extra-virgin olive oil

¼ cup (1 oz/30 g) ground pepper

8 paper-thin slices prosciutto

**FOR *the* CANDIED
GRAPEFRUIT ZEST**

1 grapefruit, preferably organic

½ cup (4 oz/125 g) sugar

FOR *the* PARSNIP PURÉE

4 Tbsp (2 oz/60 g) unsalted butter

2 or 3 shallots, minced

1½ lb (750 g) parsnips, peeled and
cut into 1-inch (2.5-cm) pieces

Kosher salt

2 cups (16 fl oz/500 ml) heavy cream

Extra-virgin olive oil as needed

3 or 4 medium sea scallops
per person

Kosher salt

We set aside a full day in Italy for sampling *prosciutto di Parma*. Unfortunately, it happened to be the one day of the week when every restaurant in Parma is closed. We're eternally making up for that day, and we try to incorporate the prosciutto of both Parma and San Daniele in as many dishes as we can. The black pepper oil is also great on cheeses like *stracciatella*, in salad dressings, and drizzled on vegetables and meats.

In a small saucepan over medium-low heat, warm the olive oil until it is gently rippling and just barely simmering, or registers 180°F (82°C) on an instant-read or deep-frying thermometer. Be careful not to let it boil. Add the pepper, stir to mix well, and keep the oil at 180°F for about 5 minutes longer. Remove from the heat and let the oil cool for at least 30 minutes or up to overnight. Strain. (The pepper oil will keep indefinitely in an airtight container at room temperature.)

Preheat your oven to the lowest setting it has, preferably 150°F (65°C). Trim the excess fat from the prosciutto slices. Line a baking sheet with parchment paper and arrange the slices on the paper. Place in the oven and bake slowly until very dry and crispy, about 30 minutes (alternatively, dry in a dehydrator until crispy). Break the prosciutto into 2-inch (5-cm) shards. Set aside.

Make the candied grapefruit zest as directed for the candied lemon zest on page 84. (The leftover candied zest will keep in an airtight container at room temperature for up to 2 weeks.)

To make the parsnip purée, in a sauté pan over medium heat, melt the butter. Add the shallots and sweat until translucent, about 5 minutes. Add the parsnips and cook until softened, just a few minutes; do not allow to brown. Season with salt. Add the cream, reduce the heat to low, and simmer until the parsnips are extremely tender, about 30 minutes. Transfer the mixture to a blender or food processor and process to a silky smooth purée. Cover the blender to keep the purée warm and set aside.

When all of the elements are prepared and you are ready to cook, pour olive oil into a large sauté pan to cover the bottom. (Work in batches or use 2 pans if necessary; you do not want to crowd the scallops or they will steam instead of sear.) Eyeball the depth of the oil and add more if needed; you want it to come about one-fourth of the way up the sides of the scallops when they are added. Put the pan(s) over high heat. Pat the scallops completely dry and season liberally with salt. When the oil almost begins to smoke, place the scallops in the pan. Cook until seared to a golden brown on the first side, just a minute or two. Carefully flip and sear on the second side for a minute or two longer, depending on the thickness and size of the scallops. Transfer to a plate to drain. If you have any scallops that are especially small, then just flip them, let them sit for a second, and immediately remove them from the pan.

to ASSEMBLE Make a swoosh of the parsnip purée on each dinner plate. Place the scallops in a row on top. Nestle the prosciutto slices between the scallops. Top each scallop with a bit of the candied grapefruit zest and drizzle the pepper oil around the plate. Serve right away.

BUTTER-POACHED
LANGOUSTINE

with

LOBSTER GLACE,
PURPLE PEARL BARLEY,
SPRING PEAS,
and DILL

SERVES 4–6

2 or 3 langoustines per person

FOR *the* LOBSTER GLACE

¼ cup (2 fl oz/60 ml)
extra-virgin olive oil

Reserved langoustine shells
(from above) or shrimp shells

2 large shallots, sliced

2 carrots, peeled and chopped

¼ cup (2 oz/60 g) tomato paste

2 cups (10 oz/315 g) canned
San Marzano tomatoes,
chopped, with their juice

1 cup (8 fl oz/250 ml) brandy

A few fresh thyme sprigs

1½ cups (10½ oz/330 g)
purple pearl barley

Kosher salt

2½ cups (12½ oz/390 g)
shelled English peas

Vegetable oil for frying

5 Tbsp (2½ oz/75 g) unsalted
butter, plus ½ cup (4 oz/125 g)
for poaching

1 shallot, minced

Grated zest and juice of ½ lemon

1 cup (1 oz/30 g) small fresh dill
sprigs, roughly chopped,
plus more for garnish

¼ cup (2 fl oz/60 ml) dry
white wine

Kosher salt

2 cups (3 oz/90 g) baby
pea tendrils

The fresh peas make this another very seasonal dish. We like to use purple pearl barley from Timeless Food, a great organic grain and lentil farm in Montana; we also love their black chickpeas. The langoustine heads are too spiny to eat but have some delicious goodness inside. You can suck the head like you would a crayfish. Any extra glace will keep for up to one week in the refrigerator. Swirl in a little butter to make a delicious dip for bread.

Remove the heads of the langoustines and reserve. With scissors, snip the tail ends on the underside to release the meat and remove the tail shells. Set the shells aside for the glace. Refrigerate the heads and the tail meat while you make the glace.

To make the glace, in a large pot over medium-high heat, warm the olive oil. Add the langoustine shells and sauté with a wooden spoon, smashing them up as you stir. Add the sliced shallots and the carrots and sauté until starting to soften, about 2 minutes. Stir in the tomato paste and cook until rust colored, about 5 minutes. Add the chopped tomatoes with their juice, the brandy, and the thyme. Add 3 cups (24 fl oz/750 ml) water and bring to a simmer. Reduce the heat to medium-low and cook until the glace is rich in color and taste, and has reduced, about 1¼ hours. Strain through a fine-mesh sieve lined with cheesecloth; reheat just before serving.

Meanwhile, put the barley in a saucepan and cover with plenty of water. Stir in 2 Tbsp salt and bring to a boil. Reduce the heat to maintain a gentle simmer and cook until tender but still a little chewy, about 30 minutes. Drain well. Cover to keep warm and set aside.

Bring another saucepan of lightly salted water to a boil over high heat. Set a large bowl of ice water nearby. Add the peas to the boiling water and cook until tender, about 3 minutes. Using a slotted spoon, transfer to the ice water to stop the cooking. Drain well and set aside.

Pour vegetable oil into a small saucepan to a depth of about 1 inch (2.5 cm) and heat over high heat to 360°F (185°C). Add the reserved langoustine heads and fry until crispy, 1–2 minutes. Transfer to a paper towel to drain. Sprinkle with salt while still warm.

In a large sauté pan, melt the 5 Tbsp butter over medium heat. Add the minced shallot and sweat until translucent, about 3 minutes. Add the barley, peas, and lemon zest and juice and fold gently to mix. Add a bit of water and stir until it emulsifies with the butter. The barley should have a luscious sheen. Toss in the 1 cup dill. Taste and adjust the seasoning. Remove from the heat and cover to keep warm.

To poach the langoustine tails, in a saucepan over medium heat, melt the ½ cup butter. Stir in the wine, about 1 cup (8 fl oz/250 ml) water, and 1 Tbsp salt. Heat until steaming, or about 140°F (60°C) on an instant-read thermometer. Add the langoustine tails and cook just until no longer translucent, about 4 minutes. Using tongs, transfer immediately to a plate to drain.

to **ASSEMBLE** Spoon a mound of the barley-pea mixture in the middle of each plate. Rest 2 or 3 langoustines on top, then ladle the glace over each plate so it coats the langoustines and pools around the barley. Place a fried head on the side of each plate, facing out. Garnish with the pea tendrils and a little dill and serve right away.

POACHED HAWAIIAN
BLUE PRAWNS
with
CREAMY POLENTA, OLD BAY CROUTONS, *and* CALABRIAN CHILES

SERVES 4–6

This is our take on shrimp and grits. Hawaiian blue prawns are plump freshwater prawns that look like the love child of a shrimp and a small lobster. Here, their sweet quality mingles perfectly with the smoky heat of the Calabrian chiles. Other freshwater prawns or large shrimp can be substituted. Look for the jarred chiles online.

FOR *the* POLENTA

2 cups (16 fl oz/500 ml) whole milk

1 cup (8 fl oz/250 ml) heavy cream

1 Tbsp kosher salt

Pinch of freshly ground pepper

1 cup (5 oz/155 g) polenta or good-quality coarse-ground cornmeal

FOR *the* PRAWNS

1 shallot, chopped

1 clove garlic, chopped

2 bay leaves

2 whole cloves

1 tsp sugar

1 Tbsp kosher salt

½ cup (4 fl oz/125 ml) dry white wine

3 or 4 prawns per person

FOR *the* OLD BAY CROUTONS

4 Tbsp (2 oz/60 g) unsalted butter

1 Tbsp Old Bay seasoning

About ½ lb (250 g) brioche or white bread loaf, crust removed, cut into 1-inch (2.5-cm) cubes

Kosher salt

1 bunch green onions, white and tender green parts, thinly sliced on the diagonal

⅓ cup (1½ oz/45 g) chopped Calabrian chiles or chile paste

To make the polenta, in a saucepan over medium heat, whisk together the milk, cream, salt, and pepper. When the mixture starts steaming (but is not boiling), slowly pour in the polenta, whisking vigorously. Cook, stirring, until the mixture begins to thicken, about 10 minutes. Cook for another minute or so, remove from the heat, cover, and let sit for 30–40 minutes.

When the polenta is almost done, make the prawns: In a pot, combine the shallot, garlic, bay leaves, cloves, sugar, salt, wine, and 2½ cups (20 fl oz/625 ml) water. Heat over medium-high heat just until the water is barely simmering, or until it registers about 160°F (71°C) on an instant-read thermometer.

While the water is heating, remove the prawns from the fridge to take the chill off, then make the croutons: In a sauté pan over medium heat, melt the butter with the Old Bay seasoning, stirring to mix well. Add the bread cubes and cook, turning as needed, until golden brown on all sides, about 10 minutes total. Transfer to paper towels to drain and season with a bit of salt.

Add the prawns to the poaching liquid and cook just until pink and opaque, about 2 minutes. Drain immediately.

When ready to serve, warm the polenta until heated through, adding a little more cream or milk if it has stiffened up too much. It should have a creamy pudding consistency. Taste and adjust the seasoning.

to ASSEMBLE Put a heaping scoop of polenta in individual shallow soup bowls or onto dinner plates. Tuck the prawns into the polenta and scatter a few croutons around the plate. Garnish with a sprinkling of green onion and chiles and serve right away.

ARCTIC CHAR

with

TOMATO-BRAISED
ROMANO BEANS *and*
MUSTARD-GLAZED
BACON

SERVES 4–6

Using a good-quality smoky bacon will make the romano beans taste like delicious Italian baked beans. Tend them closely as they cook; they should have a lot of love and soul. Arctic char is one of our favorite types of fish to serve in the cooler months. The key to getting crispy skin on fish is to have a smoking-hot pan with a good amount of oil in it, and to start with a dry piece of fish—don't salt until it is seconds away from going in the pan.

FOR *the* ROMANO BEANS

2 Tbsp extra-virgin olive oil

4 slices bacon, cut into ½-inch (12-mm) pieces

1 red onion, cut into julienne

4 cloves garlic, thinly sliced

1 Tbsp grated orange zest

1 Tbsp red pepper flakes

1 cup (8 fl oz/250 ml) dry white wine

1 can (28 oz/875 g) crushed San Marzano tomatoes

2 Tbsp red wine vinegar

1 Tbsp Worcestershire sauce

1 heaping Tbsp brown sugar

2 Tbsp chopped fresh thyme

2 Tbsp kosher salt

1 bay leaf

4 hefty handfuls of romano beans, ends trimmed

FOR *the* MUSTARD-GLAZED BACON

4–6 slices bacon

¼ cup (3 oz/90 g) maple syrup

¼ cup (2 oz/60 g) Dijon mustard

Kosher salt and freshly ground pepper

½ cup (4 fl oz/125 ml) extra-virgin olive oil

4–6 skin-on Arctic char or Tasmanian sea trout fillets, about 5 oz (155 g) each

Kosher salt

2 Tbsp unsalted butter

Preheat the oven to 350°F (180°C).

To make the romano beans, in a saucepan over medium heat, warm the olive oil. Add the bacon and fry until the fat is partly rendered and the bacon is translucent, about 3 minutes. Add the onion and sweat until softened, about 5 minutes. Stir in the garlic, orange zest, and red pepper flakes and cook for another minute or two. Pour in the wine and deglaze the pan, stirring to scrape up any browned bits from the pan bottom, then add the tomatoes. Give a good stir and begin to simmer gently. Add the vinegar, Worcestershire sauce, brown sugar, thyme, salt, and bay leaf and stir to mix well. Simmer this mixture to reduce a bit, about 7 minutes. Give it a taste. The pungency of the wine and vinegar should have calmed down by this point. If not, simmer for another minute or two. Add the beans, stir to immerse in the liquid, and reduce the heat to medium-low. Braise until tender, about 25 minutes.

While the beans are braising, make the mustard-glazed bacon: Fit a baking sheet with a rack and arrange the bacon slices on the rack, lining them up like soldiers. Place a piece of parchment paper on top, and place another baking sheet on top of the paper. (You want the bacon slices to be as flat as possible for glazing.) Pop the whole setup in the oven to begin to render the fat. Meanwhile, in a bowl, whisk together the maple syrup, mustard, and a pinch each of salt and black pepper. Have a pastry brush handy. When the bacon fat is about 85 percent rendered and the bacon is starting to crisp on the edges, you are ready to glaze. Slide the pans out of the oven, remove the top pan and the paper, and brush the bacon liberally with the mustard mixture. Put back in the oven, uncovered, and bake until the bacon is crisp and the glaze has caramelized, about 4 minutes longer. Watch closely, as it can burn easily. Remove from the oven and let cool to room temperature. Cut on the diagonal into 2-inch (5-cm) pieces. Set aside.

In a large sauté pan, warm the olive oil over high heat until almost smoking. Pat the fish fillets dry and season liberally with salt. Carefully place the fillets, skin side down, in the hot oil. Using 2 large spatulas, press on the fish for a moment so the fillets do not curl up. (You can also just use your hands, a grill press, or the bottom of a clean pan.) Once the fish will remain flat, you can remove the pressure. Reduce the heat to medium. This type of fish is best served medium-rare, so hover over it now. Cook for just 2–3 minutes longer, depending on the thickness. Remove from the heat, carefully flip the fish with your spatulas, and let sit for a moment while you plate the beans.

to ASSEMBLE Swirl the butter into the beans for some added richness. Scoop the warm beans into shallow soup bowls or onto dinner plates. Top with a few pieces of the glazed bacon. Rest a fillet on top of each portion of beans and top with more bacon. Serve right away.

GOLDEN
TILEFISH
with

SHIITAKE CREMA, CRISPY MUSHROOMS, *and* GLAZED SPRING VEGETABLES

SERVES 4–6

Tilefish has a crustacean-based diet that makes it slightly sweet and very tender. Mahimahi, opa (moonfish), and ono (wahoo) would work well here, too. The light, mild meat is the perfect canvas for all of spring's beautiful baby vegetables. Mushrooms are a great way of adding a rich meatiness to a dish. The crispy shiitakes used here are a vegetarian's answer to bacon lardons. Rehydrated dried shiitakes would work, as well.

FOR *the* CRISPY MUSHROOMS

¾ lb (375 g) shiitake mushrooms, stemmed and very thinly sliced

½ cup (4 fl oz/125 ml) olive oil

Kosher salt

FOR *the* SHIITAKE CREMA

3 Tbsp olive oil

2 large shallots, thinly sliced

3 cloves garlic, thinly sliced

1 lb (500 g) shiitake mushrooms, stemmed and coarsely chopped

Grated zest and juice of ½ orange and ½ lemon

½ cup (4 fl oz/125 ml) dry white wine

¾ cup (6 fl oz/180 ml) heavy cream

Kosher salt and freshly ground pepper

FOR *the* GLAZED VEGETABLES

1 bunch *each* baby turnips, radishes, and young carrots

1 cup (1 oz/30g) fresh basil leaves

½ cup (4 oz/125 g) unsalted butter

1 cup (2 oz/60 g) asparagus tips

Juice of 1 lemon

2 Tbsp fresh orange juice

2 Tbsp sugar

Kosher salt and freshly ground pepper

½ cup (4 fl oz/125 ml) olive oil, plus more for drizzling

4–6 skin-on golden tilefish fillets, about 5 oz (155 g) each

To make the crispy mushrooms, preheat the oven to 250°F (120°C). Line a baking sheet with parchment paper. Spread the shiitake slices on the prepared pan and drizzle with the olive oil. Bake until slightly golden and crispy, about 15 minutes. Keep an eye on them because they can burn quickly and become bitter, much like nuts. (If you have a dehydrator, finish the mushrooms off in it for a couple more hours to achieve extreme crispy goodness.) Sprinkle with salt while still warm and set aside.

To make the shiitake crema, in a sauté pan over medium heat, warm the olive oil. Add the shallots and garlic and sauté for a few minutes. When they have softened and started to take on a tiny bit of color, add the chopped shiitakes and sauté for about 4 minutes. Add the citrus zests and juices and the wine. Cook until the mixture is almost dry, about 10 minutes. Remove from the heat and transfer to a blender. Turn the machine on high. With the machine running, drizzle in the cream and blend until the crema is the consistency of sour cream. Transfer to a bowl and season with salt and pepper. Set aside.

To make the glazed vegetables, peel and quarter the turnips, trim and quarter the radishes, and peel and quarter the carrots, then slice them thinly on the diagonal. Cut the basil into chiffonade. In a large sauté pan over medium heat, melt the butter. Add the asparagus, turnips, radishes, and carrots and reduce the heat to medium-low. Sauté the vegetables for a few minutes, being careful not to let them brown. Add the lemon and orange juices, the sugar, and a splash or two of water and stir well. Simmer, stirring occasionally, until the liquid reduces to a shiny glaze, about 10 minutes. Season with salt and pepper and toss in the basil.

Just before serving, in another large sauté pan, heat ½ cup olive oil over high heat until smoking. Pat the fillets dry and season liberally with salt. Carefully place the fillets, skin side down, in the hot oil, and cook until the skin is crispy, about 2 minutes. When the skin releases from the pan, using a large, wide spatula, flip the fillets and remove from the heat. Let cook for a moment longer in the residual heat of the pan, then transfer to a platter.

to ASSEMBLE Warm the shiitake crema gently in a small sauté pan over low heat. Make a swoosh of the crema on each dinner plate. Place a mound of the vegetables on the crema and rest a fillet on top. Garnish with a drizzle of olive oil and the crispy mushrooms and serve right away.

PAN-SEARED
MACKEREL
with
VIDALIA–PINE NUT PURÉE, PICKLES, *and* APRICOTS

SERVES 4–6

This is Emma's favorite fish dish in the book. In terms of texture and flavor, it has a little of everything: sweetness from the apricot, tartness from the pickles, creaminess from the purée, and meatiness from the fish. Mackerel is a versatile and meaty fish. Play around with different types of mackerel—Atlantic, King, Spanish—to see how the dish changes.

FOR *the* VIDALIA–PINE NUT PURÉE

3 Tbsp unsalted butter

1 large Vidalia onion, cut into small dice (about 2 cups/10 oz/315 g)

¾ cup (4 oz/125 g) pine nuts, toasted

Large pinch of grated lemon zest

¼ cup (2 fl oz/60 ml) dry white wine

Splash of heavy cream

Pinch of sugar

Kosher salt

3 Tbsp extra-virgin olive oil

4–6 skin-on Spanish mackerel fillets, about 5 oz (155 g) each

Kosher salt

1 cup (8 oz/250 g) pickled fennel (see page 232)

½ cup (3 oz/90 g) pickled serrano chiles (see page 232)

1 cup (8 oz/250 g) pickled radishes (see page 232)

1 cup (6 oz/185 g) sliced fresh apricots (about 6 apricots)

Extra-virgin olive oil for drizzling

Small fresh dill sprigs for garnish

To make the vidalia–pine nut purée, in a sauté pan over medium heat, melt the butter. Add the onion and sweat until translucent and soft, about 5 minutes. Add the pine nuts and lemon zest and cook for 1 minute. Drizzle in the wine and deglaze the pan, stirring to scrape up any browned bits from the pan bottom. Simmer until the liquid is reduced by half, 2–3 minutes. Transfer to a blender and process until smooth. Add the cream, just to thin slightly, and the sugar and pulse to blend. Taste and season with salt. Set aside at room temperature.

Just before you are ready to serve, in a large sauté pan, warm the olive oil over high heat until lightly smoking. Pat the fillets completely dry and season liberally with salt. Carefully place the fillets, skin side down, in the hot oil and cook until the skin is crispy, about 2 minutes. When the skin releases from the pan, using a large, wide spatula, flip the fillets and remove from the heat. Let cook for a moment longer in the residual heat of the pan, then drain the cooking liquid.

to **ASSEMBLE** In a bowl, toss together all the pickles and apricots. Make a swoosh of the vidalia–pine nut purée on each dinner plate. Place a fish fillet on the purée and then artfully arrange the pickles and apricot slices on top of the fish. Garnish with a drizzle of olive oil and the dill and serve right away.

CONTORNI

Brussels Sprouts with Bacon, Apple, and Mustard 180

Maple-Roasted Turnips with Crème Fraîche, Hazelnuts, and Bonito 182

Picnic Potatoes 183

Piemontese Spinach 185

Creamy Polenta 185

Cheesy White Beans 186

Crispy Fingerlings with Garlic-Cayenne Aioli, Speck, and Green Onions 189

Spicy Eggplant with Mint, Peanuts, and Chile 190

Semolina Fritte with Macerated Shallots 193

We like sides. In fact, we like them so much that when we are

eating out, we sometimes choose our mains based on the sides that

are accompanying them. We like to keep the sides separate at Sorella,

because it gives our diners more control over what they eat. The dishes

in this chapter all make great accompaniments to proteins, or you

can just cook up a bunch of them for a meal. After all, vegetarians

do that very thing all the time. At Sorella, we focus on making our

sides really tasty. They are as complex in flavor as our *qualcosina*

offerings, embracing both tradition and innovation.

BRUSSELS SPROUTS

with

BACON, APPLE, *and* MUSTARD

SERVES 4–6

When we first opened, there was a lot of competition swirling around Brussels sprouts in New York City restaurants. Everyone had a signature version. Here's our take, which has been on the menu since the first day. There is something about adding crisp bacon lardons to vegetables that makes them hard to resist.

FOR *the* DRESSING

2½ Tbsp Dijon mustard

3 Tbsp red wine vinegar

1 cup (8 fl oz/250 ml) grapeseed oil

1 small shallot, minced

1 tsp mustard seeds

½ lb (250 g) slab bacon,
cut into ½-inch (12-mm) lardons

Vegetable oil for deep-frying

Rendered bacon fat or olive oil
for sautéing

2 apples, peeled, halved, cored,
and cut into small dice
(we love Honeycrisp)

2 lb (1 kg) Brussels sprouts,
ends trimmed and halved lengthwise,
or quartered if really big

Kosher salt

To make the dressing, combine the mustard and vinegar in a blender. Turn the blender on medium and slowly drizzle in the oil. Blend until the dressing is creamy and emulsified. If it breaks, add a little water and buzz it back together. Add the shallot and mustard seeds and pulse to mix. Set aside.

In a frying pan, cook the bacon over medium heat until it is crispy. Using a slotted spoon, transfer to paper towels to drain. You can use a little of the fat for sautéing the apples, then store the remainder for other uses.

Pour vegetable oil into a deep fryer or a deep saucepan to a depth of 6 inches (15 cm) and heat to 360°F (185°C).

Meanwhile, in a large sauté pan over medium heat, warm a dab of reserved bacon fat or a drizzle of olive oil. Add the apples, sauté until golden, then add the bacon lardons.

Stand back and gently place a batch of the sprouts in the hot oil. If the oil is the proper temperature, this will make a lot of noise. Make sure not to crowd them in the pan; you want the sprouts to fry, not steam, and to brown evenly. Fry until golden brown and crispy, about 10 minutes. Using a slotted spoon or wire skimmer, transfer to the pan with the apples. Repeat to cook the remaining Brussels sprouts, always allowing to oil to return to 360°F (185°C) before adding the next batch.

Toss the contents of the sauté pan to mix well. At this point, season with salt with a deft hand, as you would French fries. Scrape into a serving bowl, drizzle the dressing on top, and serve.

MAPLE-ROASTED TURNIPS

—— *with* ——

CRÈME FRAÎCHE, HAZELNUTS, *and* BONITO

—— SERVES 4–6 ——

We are big fans of Tokyo turnips, also known as Hakurei turnips. They taste like a cross between an apple and a daikon radish: crunchy, sweet, and just barely bitter. You can eat them raw or cooked, and don't be afraid to sauté the tender greens. If you can't find them, use radishes instead. The bonito flakes, shavings of smoked and dried fish related to tuna, add an earthy salinity to any dish and can also be used to flavor stock.

½ cup (2½ oz/75 g) hazelnuts

15–20 Tokyo turnips, trimmed and quartered

Extra-virgin olive oil for drizzling

Kosher salt

½ cup (5½ fl oz/170 g) pure maple syrup

¾ cup (6 oz/185 g) crème fraîche

Grated zest and juice of 1 lemon

½ cup (1 oz/30 g) bonito flakes

Preheat the oven to 350°F (180°C).

Spread the hazelnuts on a baking sheet and toast in the oven until they darken a little and the skins start to blister, 10–15 minutes. Pour the hot nuts onto a clean kitchen towel, gather up the corners, let steam for 1 minute, then rub vigorously in the towel to remove the skins. Chop roughly and set aside. Leave the oven on.

Pour the turnips onto the same baking sheet. Drizzle them with olive oil, sprinkle with salt, and toss to coat. Roast until tender, about 30 minutes. Add the maple syrup and toss to coat. Turn up the oven at the end to get some color on the turnips and reduce the syrup to a sticky glaze.

While the turnips are roasting, in a small bowl, stir together the crème fraîche and lemon zest. Add a pinch of salt and mix well. Set aside.

When ready to serve, make a swoosh of the maple crème fraîche in the middle of each plate and mound the turnips on top. Squeeze the lemon juice over the turnips, scatter the hazelnuts and bonito on top, and serve right away.

CONTORNI

PICNIC POTATOES

SERVES 8–10

This side was inspired by Japanese potato salad. We originally served it with tempura-fried quail (see note page 162), then realized it goes well with any protein and is great on its own. It's kind of a cross between potato salad and coleslaw, with the consistency of lumpy mashed potatoes.

Kosher salt

2½ lb (1.25 kg) red potatoes

½ lb (250 g) bacon

1 cup (5 oz/155 g) peeled and very thinly sliced carrots

1 cup (5 oz/155 g) very thinly sliced white onions

1 cup (4 oz/125 g) julienned green cabbage

1 cup (3 oz/90 g) julienned green onions, including tender green tops

⅓ cup (1½ oz/45 g) sesame seeds, toasted

1½ cups (12 fl oz/375 ml) good-quality mayonnaise (Japanese brand Kewpie mayonnaise is a good choice)

¼ cup (2 fl oz/60 ml) rice vinegar

Bring a saucepan of salted water to a boil over high heat. Add the potatoes and boil until extremely tender and falling apart, about 25 minutes. Drain well and transfer to a large bowl. Using a wooden spoon, mash the potatoes until they verge on resembling what you would serve as lumpy mashed potatoes. Let cool completely.

Meanwhile, in a large frying pan, cook the bacon until chewy and not too crispy. Using a slotted spoon, transfer to paper towels to drain and cool (reserve the bacon fat for another use). Cut the bacon into small pieces.

When the potatoes are cool, add the carrots, white onions, cabbage, green onions, bacon, sesame seeds, mayonnaise, and vinegar. Mix thoroughly with your hands until the salad has the consistency of creamy lumpy mashed potatoes. Taste and season with salt. Serve lightly chilled (not cold) or at room temperature.

PIEMONTESE
SPINACH

SERVES 4–6

Piemontese cooks find ways to incorporate canned fish items into recipes to add depth and salinity. This dish, which comes from the excellent *Nonna Genia's Classic Langhe Cookbook*, is a perfect example. It is also one of the best-smelling dishes in the book.

4 Tbsp (2 oz/60 g) unsalted butter

6 oil-packed anchovy fillets

5 cloves garlic, thinly sliced

2½ lb (1.25 kg) baby spinach

Juice of 1½ large lemons

Kosher salt and freshly ground pepper

In a large sauté pan over medium heat, melt the butter. Add the anchovies and garlic and sauté until the anchovies have broken down and the butter has browned, about 3 minutes. Add the spinach and sprinkle in the lemon juice. Cook just until wilted, using your spoon to push the unwilted leaves to the bottom of the pile. Season to taste with salt and pepper and serve right away.

CREAMY
POLENTA

SERVES 6–8

This everyday polenta is amazing as a base for meat or fish or as a stand-alone dish to dress up. Gorgonzola, stewed tomatoes, fresh herbs, or a Bolognese *ragù* are all tasty additions to fold into the seductive creaminess. White truffles, too.

2 cups (16 fl oz/500 ml) whole milk

2 cups (16 fl oz/500 ml) heavy cream, plus more for thinning if needed

Kosher salt and freshly ground pepper

Pinch of freshly grated nutmeg

2 cups (10 oz/315 g) polenta or good-quality cornmeal

In a saucepan over medium heat, whisk together the milk, cream, 2 Tbsp salt, pepper to taste, and the nutmeg. When the mixture starts to simmer (but not boil), slowly pour in the polenta while whisking vigorously. Continue to whisk until the polenta begins to thicken, 7–9 minutes. Cook for another minute or so, then remove from the heat, cover tightly, and let stand for about 20 minutes.

When ready to serve, gently reheat the polenta over medium-low heat, adding a little more cream (or milk) if it has stiffened up too much. It should be the consistency of creamy pudding. Serve hot.

CHEESY
WHITE BEANS

These cheesy, herby Tuscan-style beans are delicious and versatile. They can be folded into pasta, made into soup, served with meat and sautéed greens, or eaten on their own.

FOR *the* BEANS

2 cups (14 oz/440 g) dried white beans, picked over for grit and stones and soaked in cold water to cover overnight

3 qt (3 l) water, chicken stock, or a combination

1 large carrot, peeled and chopped

1 yellow onion, chopped

1 rib celery, chopped

4 cloves garlic, sliced

A few bay leaves

A hefty pinch of kosher salt

½ cup (4 fl oz/125 ml) extra-virgin olive oil

1 Tbsp red pepper flakes

5 cloves garlic, chopped

¼ cup (⅓ oz/10 g) chopped fresh rosemary

¼ cup (⅓ oz/10 g) chopped fresh sage

¼ cup (⅓ oz/10 g) chopped fresh thyme

¼ lb (125 g) pecorino cheese, grated (about 1 cup)

¼ lb (125 g) Parmesan cheese, grated (about 1 cup)

Kosher salt and freshly ground pepper

To make the beans, drain them thoroughly and put them in a large pot. Add the water or stock. Place the carrot, onion, celery, garlic, and bay leaves in a cheesecloth sachet, tie securely, and put in the pot with the beans. Throw in the salt. Bring to a boil over high heat, then reduce the heat and simmer until the beans are extremely tender, almost to the point of falling apart, about 1½ hours. Remove from the heat and let the beans cool in the liquid. Discard the sachet.

In a large sauté pan over medium heat, warm the olive oil. Add the red pepper flakes, garlic, and herbs and sauté until fragrant, about 1 minute. Drain the beans, reserving about 2 cups (16 fl oz/500 ml) of the cooking liquid. Add the beans and reserved liquid to the sauté pan and bring to a simmer. When the liquid begins to evaporate, reduce the heat to very low. Fold in the cheeses and stir until a shiny, emulsified sauce forms. Season with salt and pepper. Serve right away.

CRISPY FINGERLINGS

with

GARLIC-CAYENNE AIOLI, SPECK, *and* GREEN ONIONS

SERVES 6–8

Our love for potatoes runs deep. There have been many renditions of the crispy potato side at Sorella. All have used the same cooking method, but the garnish often changes. This recipe was the very first version, and we always seem to find our way back to it. You can have fun and come up with your own garnish, or just serve the potatoes on their own. They make for killer breakfast potatoes.

Kosher salt

2½ lb (1.25 kg) fingerling potatoes

Vegetable oil for deep-frying

2 Tbsp extra-virgin olive oil

¼ lb (125 g) speck, cut into julienne

1 cup (3 oz/90 g) thinly sliced green onions, including tender green tops, plus more for garnish

1 cup (8 fl oz/250 ml) Garlic-Cayenne Aioli (page 231)

Bring a large pot of salted water to a boil. Add the potatoes and boil until fork-tender, about 30 minutes. Drain, let cool slightly, and break up into large chunks. (The more crumbly they are, the crispier they will be once they are fried.) Set aside.

When ready to serve, pour vegetable oil into a deep saucepan or deep-fryer to a depth of 6 inches (15 cm) and heat over high heat to 360°F (185°C).

Meanwhile, in a large sauté pan over medium heat, warm the olive oil. Add the speck and green onions and sauté until the onions are tender and the speck is crispy, about 4 minutes. Keep hot.

Working in batches, add the potato chunks to the hot oil and fry until golden brown and crispy, about 4 minutes. Using a slotted spoon or wire skimmer, transfer to paper towels to drain. Repeat to cook the remaining potatoes, always allowing the oil to return to 360°F (185°C) before adding the next batch.

Add the potatoes to the sauté pan and toss and stir to mix everything together. Season with salt and transfer to a serving bowl. Drizzle a good amount of aioli on top and garnish with more green onions. Serve right away.

SPICY
EGGPLANT
with

MINT, PEANUTS, *and* CHILE

SERVES 4–6

4 Japanese eggplants, trimmed and cut into 2-inch (5-cm) pieces

Kosher salt

2 Tbsp extra-virgin olive oil

All-purpose flour for dusting

¾ cup (1 oz/30 g) chopped fresh mint

¾ cup (4 oz/125 g) unsalted roasted peanuts, chopped

1 tsp seeded and minced habanero or Thai bird chile

3 Tbsp fresh orange juice

A few splashes of rice vinegar

The eggplant in this flavorful dish should have a nice crispy sear. Draw out as much of the vegetable's moisture as you can before cooking. This process is called "degorging," which sounds sort of violent but really just involves applying a generous amount of salt to the raw eggplant slices and allowing the excess moisture to sweat to the top, tempering any bitterness and ensuring a crisp finish.

Put the eggplants in a medium bowl. Sprinkle with 1 Tbsp or so of salt to draw out the moisture and season the eggplant. Let stand for about 15 minutes.

Pour the olive oil into a large sauté pan and get it very hot. Put a small scoop of flour in a large bowl. Dry the eggplant pieces with paper towels, then add to the bowl and toss to dust with the flour. Shake off any excess flour, then add the pieces to the hot pan and fry, turning as needed, until golden and crispy on all sides, about 6 minutes total. Be careful not to let them burn or they will be bitter.

When all of the eggplant is crispy, transfer to a clean large bowl. Add the mint, peanuts, chile, orange juice, and vinegar and toss to mix well. Serve right away.

SEMOLINA FRITTE

with

MACERATED SHALLOTS

We first had these luscious salty-sweet fried cakes in Cuneo, near Asti, and for the life of us, we couldn't figure out what they were. The texture was like deep-fried lemon curd: hot, puddinglike goodness in a crispy shell. What it is, in fact, is slightly sweetened semolina custard made with lots of lemon zest and fried until the skin crackles and the inside melts.

FOR *the* MACERATED SHALLOTS

7 shallots, minced

¼ cup (2 fl oz/60 ml) white wine vinegar

¼ cup (2 oz/60 g) sugar

1 Tbsp kosher salt

Extra-virgin olive oil for greasing the pan and for drizzling

12 egg yolks

5 cups (40 fl oz/1.25 l) whole milk

Grated zest of 4 small lemons

½ cup (4 oz/125 g) sugar

3 Tbsp kosher salt

1 cup (5½ oz/170 g) plus 1 Tbsp semolina flour, plus more for dusting

5 large egg whites, whisked

Canola oil for deep-frying

Sliced green onions, including tender green tops, for garnish

To make the shallots, in a bowl, toss together the shallots, vinegar, sugar, and salt. Set aside. The shallots will turn a candy pink color and get more delicious as they stand.

When you're ready to make the fritters, have all of your ingredients and equipment ready, because once this recipe gets started, it moves quickly.

Line a 12-by-17-inch (30-by-43-cm) rimmed baking sheet with parchment paper, allowing it to overlap the rim on each side by about 5 inches (13 cm). Grease the paper with olive oil. Put the egg yolks in a heatproof bowl and set aside. Whisk together the milk, lemon zest, sugar, and salt in a medium saucepan. Warm the mixture over medium heat and taste it. It should be as sweet as it is salty. Add a little more sugar or salt if needed.

When the milk mixture starts to steam (but not boil), pour in the 1 cup (5½ oz/170 g) semolina, whisking the entire time. When the mixture starts to resemble runny Cream of Wheat, reduce the heat to low.

Ladle some of the hot semolina mixture into the egg yolks and whisk it in; repeat two more times. Add the tempered eggs to the semolina mixture in the saucepan, still whisking. Return the heat to medium and heat, whisking constantly, until the mixture reaches a boil. Keep boiling for another minute while stirring vigorously to set the eggs, then remove from the heat. Taste to check the seasoning. At this point, you can add more salt, sugar, or lemon zest, if you like.

Pour the semolina into the prepared baking sheet and spread in an even layer. Drizzle with a little olive oil and fold over the parchment to cover the semolina. Refrigerate until the mixture is completely set, about 4 hours. (You can make the fritters to this point up to 4 days ahead.)

When the semolina is set, it will be ultraspongy and firm, similar to polenta. Now you can cut it into any shape you want—we like tea-sandwich-size triangles.

Pour canola oil into a deep saucepan to a depth of about 4 inches (10 cm) and heat to 360°F (185°C). Put the egg whites into a shallow bowl, and then put a big handful of semolina into a second shallow bowl.

Dip each semolina custard piece into the egg whites, then dredge it in the semolina and slide it carefully into the hot oil. Add as many at one time as you can without crowding the pan and fry until crispy and ever so slightly golden, about 5 minutes. Using a wire skimmer, transfer to paper towels to drain, then sprinkle with a little salt while still warm. Repeat with the remaining semolina custard pieces, always allowing the oil to return to 360°F (185°C) before adding the next batch.

To serve, arrange the fritters on plates and spoon the shallots alongside. Garnish with the green onions and serve right away.

DOLCI & PANI

Bicerin 198

Amaretti Cookies 203

Almond Spritz Cookies 203

Pear Crostata with Spiced Caramel Syrup and Candied Pistachios 204

Buttermilk Gelato 207

Panna Cotta with Strawberries, Balsamic, and Amaretti 208

Hazelnut Mallomars 209

Honey-Bergamot Shortbread 210

Pine Nut–Peanut Butter and Cherry Jam Cookies 213

Marsala Torta 214

Bomboloni 217

Molly's Birthday Cake 218

Sorella Flatbread 223

English Muffin Bread 224

Buttermilk Country Bread 227

During the planning stages for Sorella, we decided not to have a pastry chef on staff. But we did hire Yarisis Jacobo to help us come up with a few desserts that Emma would be able to make easily. The two of them hit it off, and one day Emma asked, "Can I please keep her?" With Yarisis on board, we have been able to develop a killer dessert program. When three women get together and start talking sweets, magic is possible.

Making our own breads was important to us, but we didn't think we could pull it off. We thought it would be too challenging with our small team and small kitchen. Yarisis said she didn't have much experience with bread, but we think that was either a fib or she is the Doogie Howser of bread baking. We would tell her what we were trying to achieve, and she would nail it. It started with the English Muffin Bread, and it has been a delicious journey ever since. For us, bread is a vessel that enhances a dish and adds a layer of complexity and texture.

BICERIN

Here is a riff on a specialty of Turin that dates back to the eighteenth century. *Bicerin*, "small glass" in Piemontese dialect, is made by layering espresso, chocolate, and steamed milk. After trying the rich and creamy concoction at the city's Caffè al Bicerin, we were inspired to make this decadent dessert.

FOR *the* CHOCOLATE PUDDING

4 cups (32 fl oz/1 l) heavy cream

½ cup (4 oz/125 g) sugar

1 cinnamon stick

½ tsp kosher salt

8 oz (250 g) dark chocolate (61 percent cacao), chopped

1 large egg, beaten

4 Tbsp (2 oz/60 g) unsalted butter, at room temperature

FOR *the* ESPRESSO FUDGE SAUCE

4 Tbsp (2 oz/60 g) unsalted butter

⅓ cup (3 oz/90 g) light corn syrup

⅓ cup (3 oz/90 g) sugar

¼ cup (¾ oz/20 g) cocoa powder

1 Tbsp espresso powder

2 oz (60 g) milk chocolate, chopped

⅓ cup (3 fl oz/80 ml) heavy cream

1 tsp confectioners' sugar

½ tsp vanilla extract

SERVES 6–8

To make the chocolate pudding, have ready a large bowl of ice water. In a saucepan over medium heat, stir together the cream, sugar, cinnamon stick, and salt. When the mixture starts to simmer, slowly add in the dark chocolate to the hot cream mixture. Whisk to help melt the chocolate until the mixture starts to simmer again. Reduce the heat to low and slowly whisk in the egg. Continue to whisk until the custard thickens, 2–3 minutes. Remove from the heat and whisk in the butter, 1 Tbsp at a time.

Strain the custard through a fine-mesh sieve into a heatproof bowl and nestle the bowl in the ice bath. Let cool, stirring once or twice to help it along. When cool, pour into 6–8 pudding cups. Cover tightly and refrigerate until well chilled, at least 1 hour or up to 3 days.

To make the espresso fudge sauce, have ready a second large bowl of ice water. In another saucepan, combine 1 cup (8 fl oz/250 ml) water and the butter and bring to a boil over medium-high heat. Stir in the corn syrup. When the butter has melted, sift in the sugar, cocoa powder, and espresso powder and whisk to prevent any lumps. Return the mixture to a simmer and add the milk chocolate, whisking constantly to prevent the chocolate from burning. Cook until the sauce is thick and glossy, 2–3 minutes. Strain the sauce through a clean fine-mesh sieve into a heatproof bowl and nestle the bowl in the ice bath. Let cool, stirring occasionally.

to ASSEMBLE Heat the espresso fudge sauce until quite warm. Meanwhile, in a bowl, combine the cream, confectioners' sugar, and vanilla and whisk or beat with an electric mixer just until very soft peaks form. It should be almost liquid and should not hold much of a peak.

Scoop out a small spoonful of pudding from the center of each cup and drizzle some of the warm fudge sauce into each cavity, filling it. Top with the whipped cream and another drizzle of fudge sauce and serve right away.

SARAH'S *drink note* For chocolate, I always want a Brachetto d'Acqui. My favorite one is by Braida.

HOW WE HANDLE
THE END OF THE MEAL

We have always believed that the dessert course can make or break a meal. Too often it is an afterthought, especially the coffee. We have been served bad coffee in restaurants more often than we can count, so we take extra care at Sorella. We have the sexiest La Marzocco pulling beautiful shots of espresso to ensure that our coffee is on par with our dessert program.

Lots of time and lots of creativity go into producing our desserts. When we work, we like to channel our inner kid, especially when it comes to gelato. All of our flavors are like a party. For our first Valentine's Day, we put together two different menu concepts, one of them for the single woman eating at the bar. For the dessert course, we served a piece of cake, a doughnut, and a "pint of gelato"—a mini pint of salted caramel with chocolate-covered pretzels and a fudge swirl. We called the gelato Chunky Sorella, and it's been on the menu ever since. Everyone at Sorella quickly became addicted to the concept of making fun flavors reminiscent of the pints we sometimes consumed on Friday nights when we were single. Gelato became the "little star" at the end of the Sorella experience. To showcase that star, we created Stellina, our gelateria window next to Sorella, where we serve deliciously ridiculous gelato flavors.

To be women and to have an endless supply of delicious gelato is a dangerous situation that challenges our self-control every day.

AMARETTI COOKIES

These soft, chewy cookies were created to accompany our first-class espresso. We buy our beans from Counter Culture Coffee, based in North Carolina, and offer only espresso drinks, though never decaf.

8 oz (250 g) almond paste

1 cup (8 oz/250 g) sugar

2 large egg whites

MAKES ABOUT 3 DOZEN COOKIES

Preheat the oven to 350°F (180°C). Line 2 baking sheets with parchment paper.

In a stand mixer fitted with the paddle attachment, beat together the almond paste and sugar on medium speed until the almond paste is in pea-size lumps. Add the egg whites and beat until smooth.

Transfer the dough to a pastry bag fitted with a large round tip. Pipe out cookies 1–1½ inches (2.5–4 cm) in diameter on the prepared pan, spacing them about 1 inch (2.5 cm) apart. Dampen a fingertip with water and gently pat down the tip on each cookie. Bake until lightly golden, 5–8 minutes. Let cool completely on the pan on a wire rack. Load and bake the second pan the same way.

When the cookies are cool, peel them off of the paper. They will keep in an airtight container at room temperature for up to 1 week.

ALMOND SPRITZ COOKIES

We love cookies. These nutty, buttery babies go great with lots of different fruit preserves and make a perfect, easy sweet treat to serve with espresso at the end of a meal.

5 oz (155 g) almond paste

1¼ cups (10 oz/315 g) unsalted butter, at room temperature

¾ cup (6 oz/185 g) sugar

¼ tsp vanilla extract

½ tsp kosher salt

4 large egg whites, beaten

1¾ cups (7 oz/220 g) cake flour

About ½ cup (5 oz/155 g) fruit jam of choice

MAKES ABOUT 1 DOZEN COOKIES

Preheat the oven to 350°F (180°C). Line a large baking sheet with parchment paper.

In a stand mixer fitted with the paddle attachment, combine the almond paste, butter, sugar, vanilla, and salt and beat on medium speed until light and fluffy. Add the egg whites, little by little, and beat on medium speed until well mixed. On low speed, add the flour and beat just until incorporated.

Transfer the dough to a pastry bag fitted with a large star tip and chill for about 30 minutes. Pipe rosettes about 2 inches (5 cm) in diameter onto the prepared pan, working from the outside to the center in a clockwise motion to form a spiral and spacing the rosettes about 1 inch (2.5 cm) apart. Spoon a dab of the jam into the center of each rosette. Bake until the edges are lightly golden, 7–10 minutes. Let cool completely on the pan on a wire rack.

When the cookies are cool, peel them off of the paper. They will keep in an airtight container at room temperature for up to 1 week.

PEAR CROSTATA

with

SPICED CARAMEL SYRUP *and* CANDIED PISTACHIOS

We call this tasty crisp (or crumble) a *crostata*, a term more traditionally applied to an Italian fruit tart. It can be made with other fruits, is great served warm, begs for a scoop of cool, creamy gelato alongside, and includes a decadently rich caramel topping. This flavor combo is a perfect selection for a fall dessert or holiday offering.

FOR *the* CANDIED PISTACHIOS

½ large egg white

1 cup (4 oz/125 g) pistachios

¼ cup (2 oz/60 g) sugar

1 tsp kosher salt

FOR *the* STREUSEL

1 cup (8 oz/250 g) unsalted butter

½ vanilla bean, split

1½ cups (7½ oz/235 g) all-purpose flour

1 cup (7 oz/220 g) firmly packed brown sugar

1½ tsp baking soda

1 tsp baking powder

1 tsp kosher salt

¼ tsp ground cinnamon

FOR *the* FILLING

2 Tbsp unsalted butter

6 large ripe pears, peeled, cored, and sliced or chopped

¼ cup (2 oz/60 g) firmly packed brown sugar

Dash *each* of ground cinnamon, allspice, freshly grated nutmeg, and grated orange zest

Juice of ½ lemon

Pinch of kosher salt

Dash of Grand Marnier

1 tsp vanilla extract

Spiced Caramel Syrup (page 232) and gelato for serving

SERVES 6–8

To make the candied pistachios, preheat the oven to 200°F (95°C). Line a baking sheet with parchment paper or a nonstick baking mat.

In a bowl, whisk the egg white until frothy. Add the pistachios, sugar, and salt and stir to mix well. Spread the mixture on the prepared pan in a thin, even layer. Place in the oven until the mixture dries, about 20 minutes. Remove from the oven, pour the nuts onto a cutting board, and let cool. Chop roughly and set aside. Raise the oven temperature to 350°F (180°C).

To make the streusel, in a small saucepan over medium heat, begin to melt the butter. Scrape the vanilla seeds into the pan and toss in the pod. While the butter is melting, in a stand mixer fitted with the paddle attachment, combine the flour, brown sugar, baking soda, baking powder, salt, and cinnamon and stir to mix well.

Remove and discard the vanilla pod from the pan. With the mixer on low speed, slowly pour the vanilla-scented butter into the flour mixture. Continue to beat until the mixture is crumbly. Set aside.

To make the filling, in a wide saucepan over medium heat, melt the butter. Remove from the heat, add the pears, brown sugar, cinnamon, allspice, nutmeg, and orange zest, and stir and toss to coat the pears evenly. Add the lemon juice, salt, and Grand Marnier, stir to mix, and return to medium heat. Cook, stirring as needed to prevent scorching, until the pears are tender but the mixture still has lots of texture, 5–7 minutes. Remove from the heat, stir in the vanilla, and set aside to cool.

to ASSEMBLE In a medium square or rectangular baking dish or individual ramekins, spread the pear filling in an even layer. Crumble the streusel in an even layer on top. Bake until golden brown and bubbly, 20–30 minutes.

Remove from the oven and sprinkle with the candied pistachios. Let cool slightly, then cut into squares and place each square on individual plates. Top each serving with a scoop of the gelato. Drizzle with the caramel sauce and serve right away.

BUTTERMILK GELATO

When we opened Sorella, we served traditional smooth gelato. Then we got into chunkier, crazier flavors. This subtly flavored buttermilk version is meant to accompany a piece of cake or pie. It's sweet, tart, and creamy. We add fresh lemon juice to give it more tang.

1 cup (8 fl oz/250 ml) heavy cream

1 cup (8 oz/250 g) granulated sugar

1 Tbsp light corn syrup

Pinch of kosher salt

2 cups (16 fl oz/500 ml) buttermilk

¼ cup (2 fl oz/60 ml) fresh lemon juice

7 large egg yolks

MAKES ABOUT 4 CUPS
(32 FL OZ/1 L)

In a large saucepan, whisk together the cream, sugar, corn syrup, and salt. Place over medium heat, bring to a simmer, and cook, stirring occasionally, until the sugar dissolves and the mixture is hot, about 5 minutes.

Meanwhile, pour the buttermilk and lemon juice into a large heatproof bowl. Add the egg yolks and whisk until smooth. When the cream mixture is ready, gradually whisk about 1 cup (8 fl oz/250 ml) of it into the buttermilk-egg mixture. Pour the combined mixtures into the saucepan, reduce the heat to medium-low, and cook, stirring, until the custard thickens enough to coat the back of a spoon and registers 170–175°F (77–80°C) on an instant-read thermometer. Do not allow the mixture to boil or the egg yolks will curdle. Strain the custard through a fine-mesh sieve into a bowl and let cool to room temperature. (You can speed the cooling process by nestling the bowl in an ice bath and stirring from time to time.) Cover with plastic wrap and refrigerate until well chilled, at least 6 hours or up to overnight.

Pour the custard into an ice cream maker and freeze according to the manufacturer's instructions. Serve right away, or transfer to an airtight container and freeze for up to 2 weeks.

PANNA COTTA

—— *with* ——

STRAWBERRIES, BALSAMIC, *and* AMARETTI

This eggless dessert—the name translates to "cooked cream"—originated in Piedmont but is now made all over Italy. *Panna cotta* is all about texture. When the texture is right, it is silky and light yet still decadent. It is easy to dress up according to the season. We particularly like this version, which is like a sexy summer dress—no additional adornment needed.

4½ sheets gelatin

4 cups (32 fl oz/1 l) heavy cream

1 cup (8 oz/250 g) sugar

½ tsp kosher salt

1 tsp vanilla extract

3 cups (12 oz/375 g) ripe strawberries, hulled, chopped, and tossed in a little sugar

2 cups (8 oz/250 g) crumbled amaretti cookies, homemade (page 203) or store-bought

A few fresh basil leaves, cut into chiffonade

Aged balsamic vinegar for drizzling

SERVES 8–10

Soak the gelatin sheets in cold water until they are soft and pliable, about 5 minutes. Have ready a large bowl of ice water.

Meanwhile, in a saucepan, combine the cream, sugar, and salt and warm over medium heat, whisking often to dissolve the sugar, until small bubbles appear along the sides of the pan. Do not allow the mixture to boil. Immediately remove the pan from the heat. Squeeze out the excess water from the gelatin sheets and whisk the sheets into the cream mixture. Strain through a fine-mesh sieve into a heatproof bowl. Nestle the bowl in the ice bath until the mixture cools, stirring it once or twice as it cools to help it along. Stir in the vanilla.

Divide the cream mixture evenly among custard cups or ramekins, cover, and refrigerate until set, at least 2 hours or up to overnight.

to ASSEMBLE In a bowl, toss together the strawberries, cookies, and a pinch of basil. Spoon some of the strawberry mixture over each panna cotta and drizzle the balsamic vinegar over the top. Garnish with more basil and serve right away.

SARAH'S *drink note* Moscato d'Asti. Preferably Vietti. Do it.

HAZELNUT MALLOMARS

Because we grew up on mallomars and are obsessed with the chocolate-hazelnut combo, these chocolate-dipped beauties are on the Sorella menu. Unlike extracts, which have an alcohol base, the vanilla bean and praline pastes are made by infusing the flavor into a thick syrup. Look for the pastes and the sheet gelatin at specialty baking stores or online, or use powdered gelatin.

FOR *the* MARSHMALLOW CRÈME

Unsalted butter for the dish

2 cups (1 lb/500 g) sugar

¾ cup (7½ oz/235 g) corn syrup

9½ sheets gelatin

1 Tbsp vanilla bean paste

¼ cup (2½ oz/75 g) hazelnut or praline paste

FOR *the* SHORTBREAD

1½ cups (7½ oz/235 g) all-purpose flour

¼ cup (2 oz/60 g) granulated sugar

¼ cup (2 oz/60 g) firmly packed light brown sugar

⅛ tsp kosher salt

¾ cup (6 oz/185 g) very cold unsalted butter, cut into small cubes

½ vanilla bean, split lengthwise

12 oz (375 g) good-quality dark chocolate, melted for dipping

MAKES ABOUT 8 COOKIES

To make the marshmallow crème, generously butter an 8-inch (20-cm) square baking dish and set aside. In a saucepan, combine the sugar, ¾ cup (6 fl oz/180 ml) water, and about half of the corn syrup and heat to 240°F (115°C), soft-ball stage, stirring to dissolve the sugar.

While the sugar is cooking, soak the gelatin sheets in cold water until they are soft and pliable, about 5 minutes. Squeeze out the excess water and place the sheets in the bowl of a stand mixer fitted with the whisk attachment. Add the rest of the corn syrup and the vanilla bean paste to the gelatin. When the sugar syrup has reached the right temperature, with the mixer running on medium-low speed, slowly pour it into the gelatin mixture and whisk until the mixture is white, fluffy, and tripled in volume, increasing the speed to high as the mixture thickens, about 15 minutes. Beat in the hazelnut paste just until evenly incorporated. Pour into the prepared baking dish. Spread the top smooth with a rubber spatula, cover lightly with plastic wrap, and let the marshmallow set, about 1 hour.

To make the shortbread, in a food processor or the stand mixer fitted with the paddle attachment, combine the flour, granulated sugar, brown sugar, and salt and pulse or beat to mix. Scatter in the cold butter and scrape in the vanilla seeds. Discard the pod. Process or beat on medium speed just until the ingredients are incorporated and a rough mass forms. Pat the dough into a disk, wrap in plastic wrap, and refrigerate until chilled, at least 1 hour or up to 1 week.

Preheat the oven to 350°F (180°C). Line a baking sheet with parchment paper.

On a lightly floured work surface, roll out the shortbread dough ¼ inch (6 mm) thick. Using a 3-inch (7.5-cm) fluted round cookie cutter, cut out rounds. (It's best not to gather up scraps to make more rounds; the more you work this dough, the tougher it becomes.) Arrange on the prepared baking sheet and bake until lightly golden, about 3 minutes. Rotate the pan and bake until evenly golden, another 3 minutes. Remove from the oven, let cool for about 5 minutes on the pan, then transfer to a wire rack to cool completely.

***to* ASSEMBLE** Using the same cookie cutter, cut out circles of marshmallow to match the shortbread. You'll want equal amounts of cookies and marshmallows, or at least 8 of each. Stick the marshmallow rounds to the shortbread rounds. (You may need to dampen the marshmallow with a fingertip dipped in water for a good seal.)

Dip the marshmallow-shortbread stacks in the melted chocolate and place on a wire rack to dry. The cookies will keep in an airtight container at room temperature or in the refrigerator for up to 2 weeks.

HONEY-BERGAMOT
SHORTBREAD

Our friend John Magazino sells specialty goods from Italy and showed up one day with a beautiful array of citrus fruits, including bergamot. We wanted to put all of them in glass bowls and fill the dining rooms with their intoxicating smells and vibrant colors. The bergamots went missing, however. Then Yarisis debuted this shortbread. And we weren't bothered that they had disappeared.

Unsalted butter for the dish

4 cups (1¼ lb/625 g) all-purpose flour

1⅓ cups (11 oz/345 g) sugar, plus more for sprinkling

2½ tsp kosher salt

2 cups (1 lb/500 g) unsalted butter, cut into small cubes

¼ cup (3 oz/90 g) honey

Pinch of grated orange zest

A few drops of bergamot oil

MAKES ABOUT 64
1-INCH (2.5-CM) COOKIES

Preheat the oven to 325°F (165°C). Generously butter an 8-inch (20-cm) square baking dish.

In a food processor, combine the flour, sugar, and salt and pulse to mix. Add the butter cubes and toss to coat with the flour mixture and distribute evenly around the bowl. Add the honey and zest and pulse once or twice. Add a drop or two of the bergamot oil and pulse once. Add another drop if needed to make the mixture fragrant.

Pulse just until the mixture forms uniform fine crumbs that are starting to clump together. Do not overmix! Scrape into the prepared baking dish and press the dough gently to make an even layer. Prick the top of the dough all over with fork tines. This allows steam to escape during baking, so the dough will not puff up.

Bake until golden brown, 20–35 minutes. Let cool slightly, sprinkle with sugar, then cut into diamonds, squares, or any shape you like. Let cool completely before serving. The shortbread will keep in an airtight container at room temperature for up to 1 week.

PINE NUT–
PEANUT BUTTER
and
CHERRY
JAM COOKIES

The combination of peanut butter and jelly is obvious. But the addition of pine nuts? Genius. You can substitute any jam or jelly filling you would like for the cherry jam. For example, these cookies are also great with apricot jam flavored with vanilla.

FOR *the* CHERRY JAM

1 lb (500 g) cherries, pitted and chopped, or 3 cups (15 oz/470 g) frozen pitted cherries

½ cup (4 oz/125 g) sugar

1 whole star anise

1½ tsp liquid pectin

Pinch of kosher salt

2½ cups (12½ oz/390 g) all-purpose flour

½ tsp baking soda

½ tsp salt

1 cup (8 oz/250 g) unsalted butter, at room temperature

1 cup (10 oz/315 g) creamy peanut butter, at room temperature

1 cup (8 oz/250 g) granulated sugar, plus more for sprinkling

1 cup (7 oz/220 g) firmly packed dark brown sugar

2 large eggs

1½ cups (7½ oz/235 g) pine nuts, toasted

MAKES ABOUT 10 LARGE SANDWICH COOKIES

To make the jam, in a medium saucepan combine the cherries, ¼ cup (2 oz/60 g) of the sugar, and the star anise. Place over medium heat and cook, stirring to dissolve the sugar, until the cherries begin to break down and the mixture starts to boil.

In a small bowl, whisk together the pectin and the remaining ¼ cup sugar. Stir the mixture into the cherries and cook, stirring constantly, until the cherries have broken down and the mixture is jammy, about 15 minutes. Stir in the salt. Remove from the heat. Remove and discard the star anise pod. You should have about 1 cup (10 oz/315 g). You will need about half of it for the cookies. Refrigerate the remainder in a tightly capped jar for up to 3 weeks.

Preheat the oven to 350°F (180°C). Line 2 large baking sheets with parchment paper.

In a bowl, whisk together the flour, baking soda, and salt and set aside.

In a stand mixer fitted with the paddle attachment, combine the butter, peanut butter, and sugars and beat on medium speed until creamy. Add the eggs, one at a time, beating after each addition until combined, then continue to beat until the mixture is fluffy. On low speed, add the flour mixture in two or three additions and beat just until combined. Stir in the pine nuts, distributing them evenly.

Pinch off golf-ball-size pieces of dough, roll them into balls between your palms, and place on one of the prepared pans, spacing them about 1 inch (2.5 cm) apart. Flatten each ball with your palm and sprinkle the tops with granulated sugar.

Bake until golden, about 8 minutes. Remove from the oven and transfer to a wire rack to cool completely. While the first batch is baking, load the second prepared pan with the remaining dough, then bake and cool as directed.

Spread about 2 tsp of the jam on the flat side of half of the cookies. Top with the remaining cookies, flat side down. The cookies can be stored in an airtight container at room temperature for up to 1 week.

MARSALA TORTA

This dessert was inspired by the *sacripantina* cake from Stella Bakery in San Francisco. It was Emma's birthday cake from the time she was little and holds a dear place in her heart. When her family moved to the East Coast, her dad asked for the recipe but declined to pay the million-dollar price tag. He never stopped looking for another version. We described it to Yarisis, and she did a damn good job of re-creating it for our opening menu. Now it's family legend.

FOR *the* ORANGE GÉNOISE

Nonstick cooking spray

5 large eggs

¾ cup (6 oz/185 g) granulated sugar

1¾ cups (7 oz/220 g) cake flour, sifted

Grated zest of ½ orange

1 tsp vanilla extract

¼ tsp kosher salt

4 Tbsp (2 oz/60 g) unsalted butter, melted

FOR *the* MARSALA ZABAGLIONE

1 sheet gelatin, or 1 tsp powdered gelatin

5 large egg yolks

1½ cups (12 fl oz/375 ml) heavy cream

6 Tbsp (3 fl oz/90 ml) Marsala wine

¼ cup (2 oz/60 g) granulated sugar

Grated zest of ½ large orange

¼ tsp kosher salt

½ vanilla bean, split

FOR *the* ORANGE SYRUP

1 cup (8 oz/250 g) granulated sugar

Grated zest of 1 large orange

2 cups (16 fl oz/500 ml) heavy cream

1 Tbsp confectioners' sugar

½ tsp vanilla extract

MAKES ONE 8-INCH CAKE

To make the génoise, preheat the oven to 325°F (165°C). Line three 8-inch (20-cm) round cake pans with parchment paper. Spray the paper with nonstick cooking spray.

In a stand mixer fitted with the whisk attachment, whip the eggs on high speed until they start to lighten in color. Slowly add the granulated sugar in a steady stream and continue to beat on high speed until the mixture is fluffy and doubled in volume. Remove the bowl from the mixer stand and, using a rubber spatula, fold the flour into the egg mixture in three batches just until combined. Then fold in the orange zest, vanilla, salt, and butter, again mixing just until combined.

Divide the batter evenly among the prepared pans. Bake the cakes until golden brown and the tops spring back when lightly pressed with a fingertip, 18–20 minutes. Remove from the oven and immediately run a small, thin knife blade around the inside edge of each pan. Invert a wire rack on top of a cake and invert the pan and rack together. Lift off the pan and peel off the paper. Repeat with the remaining 2 cakes. Turn the cakes upright on the racks and let cool completely.

To make the zabaglione, have ready a large bowl of ice water. Soak the gelatin sheet in cold water until soft and pliable, about 5 minutes. If using powdered gelatin, sprinkle it over about 2 Tbsp water and leave to soften for 3–5 minutes. Combine the egg yolks, ½ cup (4 fl oz/125 ml) of the cream, the Marsala, granulated sugar, orange zest, and salt in a large heatproof bowl. Scrape the vanilla seeds into the bowl and toss in the pod. Whisk to combine, then place over (not touching) simmering water in a saucepan and whisk continuously until the mixture thickens and doubles in volume.

Squeeze the water out of the gelatin sheet, add to the Marsala mixture (or add the dissolved powdered gelatin), and whisk until dissolved. Strain the mixture through a fine-mesh sieve into a heatproof bowl, then nestle the bowl in the ice bath to cool.

Meanwhile, in a bowl, whisk the remaining 1 cup (8 fl oz/250 ml) cream until medium-firm peaks form. When the Marsala mixture is cool, fold in the whipped cream just until combined. Cover and refrigerate until ready to use.

To make the syrup, in a saucepan, combine the granulated sugar, orange zest, and 2 cups (16 fl oz/500 ml) water and bring to a simmer, stirring until the sugar has dissolved completely. Remove from the heat and let cool.

to ASSEMBLE Preheat the oven to 300°F (150°C). Using a serrated knife, slice the slightly domed top off of each cake, so the tops are level. Place the tops on a baking sheet and place in the oven until dry, about 15 minutes. Let cool, crumble into a food processor, and pulse until reduced to crumbs. Set aside.

Place an 8-inch (20-cm) bottomless ring mold or ring from a springform pan on a 10-inch (25-cm) cardboard cake round or directly on a serving platter. Drop in 1 cake layer, cut side up. With a pastry brush, soak the cake generously with one-third of the syrup. Top with half of the zabaglione. Add the second cake layer, cut side up, soak with half of the remaining syrup, and top with the remaining zabaglione. Top with the third cake layer, bottom side up, and soak with the remaining syrup. Cover and refrigerate overnight to set.

The next day, run a thin, sharp knife blade around the inside edge of the mold to loosen the cake sides, then gently lift off the mold. Combine the cream, confectioners' sugar, and vanilla in a bowl and beat until stiff peaks form. Spread the whipped cream on the sides and top of the cake, then dust the top and the sides with the cake crumbs. Cut into pieces and serve.

BOMBOLONI

Warm doughnuts make people smile. We fry these little Italian puffs to order at Sorella and have served them many ways: filled with various things, rolled in different sugars, and glazed. Our favorite version coats them with a vanilla glaze. Be careful when you bite into one of these filled puffs. They can squirt and be messy.

FOR *the* VANILLA SUGAR

2 cups (1 lb/500 g) granulated sugar

1 vanilla bean, split

FOR *the* DOUGH

1¼-oz (37-g) package of fresh yeast, or 1 Tbsp active dry yeast

2 Tbsp lukewarm water

1½ cups (7½ oz/235 g) bread flour

2½ Tbsp granulated sugar

½ tsp kosher salt

2 large eggs

6 Tbsp unsalted butter, at room temperature, plus more for the pan and work surface

FOR *the* LEMON CURD FILLING

½ cup (4 oz/125 g) granulated sugar

2 whole large eggs

3 large egg yolks

Grated zest of 3 lemons

½ cup (4 fl oz/125 ml) fresh lemon juice

2½ Tbsp fresh lime juice

⅓ cup (3 oz/90 g) cold unsalted butter, cut into small cubes

Vegetable oil for deep-frying

FOR *the* GLAZE

3 Tbsp unsalted butter

1 cup (3 oz/90 g) confectioners' sugar, sifted

2 Tbsp hot water

1 tsp vanilla extract

¼ tsp kosher salt

MAKES ABOUT 18 BOMBOLONI; SERVES 4–6

To make the vanilla sugar, put the sugar in an airtight plastic container. Scrape the vanilla seeds into the sugar, stir and toss the sugar to distribute the seeds evenly, and then bury the pods in the sugar, as well. Cover the container and let it sit for at least 24 hours before using, shaking it every now and again. (You will have more than you need for this recipe; the remainder will keep in a cool, dry place for months.)

To make the dough, in a small bowl, sprinkle the yeast over the lukewarm water and let stand until foamy, about 5 minutes. In a stand mixer fitted with the dough hook, combine the flour, granulated sugar, salt, eggs, and yeast mixture and beat on low speed until a dough forms and pulls away completely from the sides of the bowl, about 7 minutes. As you mix, stop the mixer regularly and scrape down the sides of the bowl. Add the butter and continue to beat, stopping to scrape down the bowl as needed, until the butter is fully incorporated and the dough once again pulls away from the sides of the bowl.

Line a large baking sheet with parchment paper and grease the paper with butter. Grease a work surface and turn the dough out onto it. Cover with plastic wrap and let rest for 10 minutes. Roll out the dough ½ inch (12 mm) thick, re-cover, and let rest for another 10 minutes. Using a 2-inch (5-cm) round biscuit cutter, cut out rounds and transfer them to the prepared pan. Cover the rounds with a kitchen towel and let rise until doubled in size, about 1 hour. If not frying right away, refrigerate until needed, then let sit at room temperature for about 10 minutes before cooking.

To make the filling, in the top pan of a double boiler, combine the sugar, whole eggs, egg yolks, lemon zest and juice, and lime juice and whisk just to combine. Place over (not touching) simmering water in the bottom pan and whisk constantly until the mixture has emulsified and falls from the whisk in wide ribbons, about 15 minutes. Remove from the heat and whisk in the butter, a few pieces at a time. Strain through a fine-mesh sieve into a heatproof bowl and let cool. You will have about 1¼ cups (10 fl oz/310 ml) lemon curd. (This filling is also great with some fresh raspberries smashed into it.) Transfer to a piping bag fitted with a small round tip.

Pour oil into a deep fryer or deep saucepan to a depth of 2 inches (5 cm) and heat to 335°F (168°C). Working in small batches to avoid crowding, add the bomboloni and fry, turning once, until golden brown on both sides, about 4 minutes total. As each batch is done, transfer to paper towels to drain.

While the bomboloni are frying, make the glaze. In a saucepan over medium heat, melt the butter. Add the confectioners' sugar and stir until well blended. Remove from the heat, add the hot water, vanilla, and salt, and stir until smooth.

Put about ¼ cup (2 oz/60 g) of the vanilla sugar in a shallow bowl. Roll about half of the hot bomboloni in the sugar, coating them evenly. Let cool slightly, then gently poke a hole into each sugar-coated puff and pipe in about 1 Tbsp of the curd. Pipe the curd into the remaining bomboloni without vanilla sugar, then dip them, one at a time, into the glaze and place on a wire rack to drain briefly. Serve all the bomboloni right away.

DOLCI & PANI

MOLLY'S
BIRTHDAY CAKE

We take dessert and birthdays seriously. And because we are a small team, we often spend our birthdays together at work. This cake was created for Molly, our sous chef at the time. It was so good we sold the leftovers as a special. And it was so popular, we put it on the menu. We serve it with a lighted candle, which can confuse people. We then explain it's Molly's birthday cake.

FOR *the* BROWNIE LAYERS

2 cups (1 lb/500 g) unsalted butter, at room temperature, plus more for the pans

8 oz (250 g) good-quality unsweetened chocolate, chopped

3½ cups (28 oz/875 g) granulated sugar

5 large eggs

2 Tbsp vanilla extract

2 tsp fine sea salt

1 cup (5 oz/155 g) all-purpose flour

FOR *the* MARSHMALLOW CRÈME

4 tsp unflavored powdered gelatin

1 cup (8 oz/250 g) granulated sugar

6 Tbsp (4 oz/125 g) light corn syrup

1½ tsp vanilla bean paste

FOR *the* CHOCOLATE FUDGE SAUCE

4 Tbsp (2 oz/60 g) unsalted butter

½ cup (4 oz/125 g) granulated sugar

½ cup (5 oz/155 ml) light corn syrup

⅓ cup (1 oz/30 g) unsweetened cocoa powder

3 oz (90 g) dark chocolate (60 percent cacao), chopped

To make the brownie layers, preheat the oven to 350°F (180°C). Grease three 9-by-2-inch (23-by-5-cm) round cake pans. Line the bottom of each pan with parchment paper and grease the paper.

Put 1 cup (8 oz/250 g) of the butter, cut into chunks, and the chocolate in the top pan of a double boiler and place over (not touching) barely simmering water in the bottom pan. Heat, stirring occasionally, until melted and smooth. Remove from the heat and set aside. In a stand mixer fitted with the paddle attachment, combine the remaining 1 cup butter and the sugar and beat on medium-high speed until fluffy, about 5 minutes. Add the eggs, one at a time, beating after each addition until combined. Beat in the vanilla and salt and then stop the mixer and scrape down the sides of the bowl. On medium speed, add the chocolate mixture and beat until well mixed, stopping to scrape down the bowl as needed. On low speed, add the flour and mix until just blended. Pour the brownie batter into the prepared pans, dividing it evenly. Bake until a toothpick inserted into the center of each brownie layer comes clean, about 30 minutes. Remove from the oven and transfer to wire racks to cool for 20 minutes. Loosen the edges with a blunt knife, if needed, and invert the brownie layers onto the racks, peel off the parchment, and let cool completely.

While the brownie layers are baking, begin making the remaining cake components. To make the marshmallow crème, in a small bowl, sprinkle the gelatin over ¼ cup (2 fl oz/60 ml) cold water and let stand until softened, about 5 minutes. Meanwhile, in a saucepan, combine the sugar, 6 Tbsp (3 fl oz/90 ml) water, and 3 Tbsp of the corn syrup. Stir to combine, place over medium heat, bring to a boil, and cook, stirring often with a heat-resistant rubber spatula, until the mixture reaches 240°F (115°C) on a candy thermometer (soft-ball stage). While the sugar is cooking, transfer the gelatin mixture to the bowl of the stand mixer and fit the mixer with the whisk attachment. Add the remaining 3 Tbsp corn syrup and the vanilla bean paste to the gelatin. When the sugar syrup is ready, with the mixer running, slowly pour the hot syrup directly over the gelatin mixture, trying not to drip it onto the sides of the bowl or directly onto the whisk. Continue to beat until the mixture is white, fluffy, and has tripled in volume, about 6 minutes. Transfer the marshmallow crème to a piping bag fitted with a large round tip or to a resealable plastic bag with a corner snipped off.

To make the chocolate fudge sauce, in a saucepan, combine the butter and 1 scant cup (7½ fl oz/235 ml) water and bring to a rolling boil over high heat. Add the sugar and corn syrup and cook, stirring, until dissolved. Reduce the heat to medium and add the cocoa powder and chocolate. Simmer, whisking constantly to prevent burning, until the sauce thickens, about 15 minutes. Let cool completely, then transfer to a second piping bag with a large round tip or a resealable plastic bag with a corner snipped off.

FOR *the* PEANUT BUTTER GANACHE

2½ oz (75 g) white chocolate, chopped

¼ cup (2½ oz/75 g) creamy natural peanut butter

¼ cup (2 fl oz/60 ml) heavy cream

2 Tbsp light corn syrup

¼ tsp vanilla extract

Pinch of kosher salt

1 cup (5 oz/155 g) almonds, toasted and chopped, plus more for garnish

2 pints (32 fl oz/1 l) good-quality chocolate gelato, softened just until spreadable

MAKES ONE 9-INCH (23-CM) CAKE;
SERVES 12–14

To make the peanut butter ganache, put the white chocolate and peanut butter in a heatproof bowl and set aside. In a saucepan over medium heat, combine the cream, corn syrup, vanilla, and salt and bring to a simmer. Cook, stirring occasionally, for 3 minutes. Remove from the heat and pour over the peanut butter and chocolate. Let cool for a few minutes, then whisk until smooth. Transfer to a third piping bag with a large round tip or a resealable plastic bag with a corner snipped off.

to ASSEMBLE THE CAKE On a sturdy, even surface such as a small baking sheet or a freezer-proof plate, place 1 brownie layer. Sprinkle about half of the almonds evenly over the layer. Spread half of the softened gelato over the almond layer. Working to create big swirls, pipe first half of the marshmallow crème, then one-third of the chocolate fudge sauce, and finally half of the peanut butter ganache over the gelato. Top with the second brownie layer and repeat the layers, using the rest of the almonds, gelato, marshmallow crème, and ganache and half of the remaining fudge sauce. (If the brownie layers begin to break, simply patch them back together. The finished cake is very forgiving.) Top with the final brownie layer and press evenly, so that all of the layers are secure. Pipe the remaining fudge sauce on top. Freeze until firm, at least 2 hours or up to overnight. Cut into slices and enjoy.

Note: You can use your own favorite fudge sauce and marshmallow crème, either store-bought or homemade (you'll need about 2 cups/16 fl oz/500 ml of each), and if you don't want to fiddle with piping bags, you can just spread them and the ganache onto the layers.

Dessert and coffee, or, in our case, espresso, are among the last impressions you leave with a guest. And if last impressions are truly lasting, what's the point of serving a great dessert if it comes with a cup of crappy coffee? And, of course, vice versa.

SORELLA FLATBREAD

This flatbread is munched on by everyone at Sorella, including us, at all hours of the day and night. It is strangely addictive in a Ritz cracker sort of way and is a great vessel for toppings. A good-quality olive oil gives the dough a rich, buttery taste. For a zingy variation, add 2 tablespoons roasted garlic paste to the dough.

1¾ cups (9 oz/280 g) all-purpose flour

1 tsp baking powder

¾ tsp kosher salt, plus ¼ cup (2 oz/60 g) salt for sprinkling

⅓ cup (3 fl oz/80 ml) extra-virgin olive oil, plus more for brushing

2 Tbsp chopped fresh flat-leaf parsley leaves

MAKES ABOUT SIX 12-INCH (30-CM) SHEETS

Preheat the oven to 425°F (220°C).

In a stand mixer fitted with the paddle attachment, combine the flour, baking powder, and the ¾ tsp salt and beat briefly to mix. Add the olive oil and parsley and beat on low speed until evenly combined. Gather the dough into a ball, wrap in plastic wrap, and let rest for 15 to 20 minutes.

Line 3 baking sheets with parchment paper.

Cut the dough into 6 equal pieces. Run a piece through a pasta machine, beginning with the widest setting and ending with the third narrowest setting. You should have an oval rectangle about 12 inches (30 cm) long and 4 inches (10 cm) wide. Lay it flat on the prepared pan. Repeat to roll out the remaining dough pieces. (The dough can also be rolled out with a rolling pin.)

When all the dough has been rolled out, brush with olive oil and sprinkle with the ¼ cup salt. (If you want to make the breads into crackers, simply transfer the sheets now to a cutting board, cut into bite-size rectangles, and return to the pan; the flatbreads can be broken into shards after baking, too.) One at a time, place a baking sheet in the oven and bake until the edges of the flatbread are golden brown, 8–10 minutes. Transfer to wire racks and let cool completely. The flatbread can be stored in an airtight container at room temperature for up to 1 week.

ENGLISH
MUFFIN BREAD

This is our take on a James Beard recipe from *Beard on Bread*. It really is incredible. You get all of the nooks and crannies that you love in English muffins, in a loaf! We like using this bread for pressed sandwiches, for toast and eggs, for garlic bread, or for simply grilling.

Vegetable oil for the pan

2 tsp active dry yeast

½ cup (4 fl oz/125 ml) warm water

2½ cups (12½ oz/390 g) all-purpose flour

1 Tbsp sugar

2 tsp kosher salt

¼ tsp baking soda

¾ cup plus 2 Tbsp whole milk (7 fl oz/220 ml)

MAKES ONE 9-BY-5-INCH (23-BY-13-CM) LOAF

Oil a 9-by-5-by-3-inch (23-by-13-by-7.5-cm) loaf pan.

In a small bowl, sprinkle the yeast over the warm water and let stand until foamy, about 5 minutes. In a stand mixer fitted with paddle attachment, combine the flour, sugar, salt, and baking soda and mix briefly.

On low speed, add the milk and the yeast mixture, then gradually increase the speed to medium, beating until all the flour is fully incorporated. Continue to beat until the dough is smooth, supple, and pulls away from the sides of the bowl.

Transfer the dough to the prepared pan, cover with a kitchen towel, and let rise in a warm spot until doubled in size, about 1 hour. Preheat the oven to 350°F (180°C).

Bake the bread until puffy and golden, about 30 minutes. Turn out of the pan onto a wire rack and let cool completely.

BUTTERMILK
COUNTRY BREAD

This bread was created for our Pork Rillette (page 57). When it is toasted, it has that perfect crunchy-outside-fluffy-inside thing going on. It's also great for all types of sandwiches, especially pressed *panini*. But do you know what this bread doesn't do? It doesn't rip up the roof of your mouth, because that's the worst.

2 tsp active dry yeast

½ cup (4 fl oz/125 ml) warm water

3 cups (15 oz/470 g) bread flour

¼ cup (2 oz/60 g) sugar

1 Tbsp kosher salt

½ cup (4 fl oz/125 ml) buttermilk

1 large egg

2 Tbsp extra-virgin olive oil, plus more for the bowl

1 large egg white

3 Tbsp whole milk

MAKES 2 LARGE RUSTIC LOAVES

In a small bowl, sprinkle the yeast over the warm water and let stand until foamy, about 5 minutes. In a stand mixer fitted with the dough hook, combine the flour, sugar, salt, buttermilk, egg, olive oil, and yeast mixture and beat on low speed until combined. Increase the speed to medium and beat until the dough is smooth and elastic and pulls away from the sides of the bowl, about 10 more minutes. Transfer the dough to an oiled bowl, cover with plastic wrap, and let the dough rise in a warm place until doubled in size, about 2 hours.

Line a baking sheet with parchment paper. Turn the dough out onto a lightly floured work surface and cut it in half. Take half and flatten it out into a rectangle about 14 inches (35 cm) long and 12 inches (30 cm) wide. Starting on the long side, roll the dough up like a jelly roll. Pinch the long seam and the ends to seal, and roll lightly to shape a large baguette-size loaf. Place on the prepared baking sheet. Repeat with the second half of the dough. Cover with plastic wrap and let rise again in a warm spot until doubled in size, about 30 minutes. After about 10 minutes, preheat the oven to 350°F (180°C).

Whisk together the egg white and milk to make an egg wash. Brush the loaves with the egg wash and bake until golden brown, about 25 minutes. Press on the loaves to make sure they have firmed up. Transfer to wire racks and let cool completely. The loaves can be stored in an airtight container at room temperature for up to 3 days.

CONDIMENTS & BASICS

Our food is flavorful. Sometimes, we use a weapon we call

a flavor bomb to add that extra something. These bombs usually

come in the form of condiments or pickles. We like the simple power

a zesty aioli has to add a bright, sumptuous quality to something fried,

or the way a sweet jam can bring out savory tastes you didn't know

existed. Here are some of the items we like to keep around,

and most of them will keep for a while, too, which makes them

especially handy. Next time you get wonton soup or Thai food

delivered, keep the plastic containers it arrived in. They are great

for stashing pickles and condiments for storage.

QUINCE AND BACON MARMALADE

MAKES ABOUT 2 CUPS (20 OZ/625 G)

¾ lb (375 g) bacon, cut into 1-inch (2.5-cm) pieces

½ cup (2 oz/60 g) sliced shallots

½ cup (1½ oz/45 g) chopped green onions, including tender green tops, plus more for garnish

6 cloves garlic, sliced

1 tsp red pepper flakes

Grated zest and juice from ½ orange

½ lb (250 g) quince paste

½ cup (3½ oz/105 g) firmly packed brown sugar

⅓ cup (3 fl oz/80 ml) red wine vinegar

In a wide, heavy saucepan or rondeau, start frying the bacon over medium heat. When it is translucent and the fat has rendered, after about 5 minutes, add the shallots, green onions, and garlic and cook for about 1 minute longer. Add the red pepper flakes, orange zest and juice, quince paste, and sugar. As the quince paste breaks down, stir the mixture to combine. Add 2 cups (16 fl oz/500 ml) water and the vinegar and stir well. Cook, stirring until the sugar dissolves, then continue to cook over medium heat, stirring often, until the mixture has reduced to the consistency of a thick barbecue sauce, about 30 minutes.

Remove from the heat and pass the mixture through a food mill fitted with the medium disk to yield a chunky texture. Let the marmalade cool, transfer to a sterilized, tightly capped jar or other airtight container, and refrigerate for up to 3 weeks. When serving, garnish with green onions.

SWEET-AND-SOUR LILIKOI

MAKES ABOUT 2 CUPS (20 OZ/625 G)

⅓ cup (3 oz/90 g) bacon fat

1 small shallot, minced

6 very ripe passion fruits (lilikoi)

2 cups (1 lb oz/500 g) sugar

1 tsp red pepper flakes

Kosher salt

Chopped fresh chives for garnish

In a heavy saucepan over medium heat, melt the bacon fat. Add the shallot, and sweat until translucent, about 3 minutes. Halve the passion fruits and scoop out the seeds and pulp into the pan. Add 2 cups (16 fl oz/500 ml) water, the sugar, the red pepper flakes, and a hefty pinch of salt. Cook, stirring, until the sugar dissolves. Continue to cook over medium heat, stirring occasionally, until a syrup forms, about 30 minutes.

Remove from the heat and transfer to a blender. Let cool, then purée on high speed until the seeds are blasted. Do not strain the purée; the seeds add a cool look and texture. Let the sauce cool, transfer to a sterilized, tightly capped jar or other airtight container, and refrigerate for up to 3 weeks. When serving, garnish with chives.

BARKER'S MUSTARD

MAKES ABOUT 2 CUPS (16 OZ/500 G)

⅔ cup (2¼ oz/70 g) dry mustard

1 Tbsp sugar

2 tsp kosher salt

3 large eggs

1 cup (8 fl oz/250 ml) malt vinegar

2 Tbsp honey

½ tsp Tabasco sauce

In a bowl, stir together the mustard, sugar, and salt until well blended. Add the eggs and whisk until smooth. Whisk in the vinegar, honey, and Tabasco. Cover and refrigerate for about 2 hours.

Transfer the mixture to the top pan of a double boiler placed over simmering water in the bottom pan and whisk until thick and creamy, 12–15 minutes. Remove from the heat, let cool, transfer to a sterilized, tightly capped jar or other airtight container, and refrigerate for up to 2 weeks.

BASIC AIOLI

MAKES ABOUT 2 CUPS (16 FL OZ/500 ML)

4 egg yolks

1½ cups (12 fl oz/375 ml) grapeseed oil

1½ tsp kosher salt

Put the egg yolks into the bowl of a food processor. Turn the processor on and process just until the eggs are blended. Very slowly drizzle in the oil until a stiff sauce forms. If you prefer a thinner aioli, with the processor running, drizzle in a little warm water until the desired consistency is achieved. Season with the salt.

Tip: Make sure there is no residue in the bowl of your food processor by wiping it with a little bit of white vinegar. A perfectly clean bowl ensures that the eggs and oil will emulsify properly.

VARIATIONS

For each of the following variations, make the Basic Aioli, then mix in the additional ingredients:

- **Lemon Aioli** Grated zest of 2 lemons, 1½ Tbsp fresh lemon juice, 1 tsp sugar

- **Orange-Cayenne Aioli** Grated zest of ½ large orange, 1½ Tbsp fresh orange juice, 1 tsp cayenne pepper, 1 tsp sugar

- **Herb Aioli** Grated zest of ½ lemon, 1½ tsp fresh lemon juice, ½ cup (4 fl oz/125 g) puréed mixed fresh herbs (basil, tarragon, chives, chervil, mint, dill), freshly ground pepper

- **Curry Aioli** Pinch *each* of grated lemon zest and orange zest, 1½ Tbsp curry powder, 1 Tbsp fresh lemon juice, pinch of ground cardamom, freshly ground pepper

- **Taggiasca Aioli** ½ cup (3 oz/90 g) Taggiasca or other dark, buttery olives, pitted and puréed until smooth; 1½ tsp fresh lemon juice; tiny pinch *each* of sugar and grated orange zest; freshly ground pepper

- **Pickled Pepper Aioli** 2 pickled habanero chiles, puréed; ½ cup (2 oz/60 g) pepperoncini, puréed; 2½ Tbsp *each* liquid from pepperoncini and habanero jars, 1½ tsp sugar (this should be a thinner aioli and spicy yet sweet)

- **Garlic–Cayenne Aioli** 2 Tbsp cayenne pepper, 10 cloves garlic mashed to a paste with 1 tsp salt, 1 tsp sugar, squeeze of lemon

APRICOT SPREAD

MAKES ABOUT 3 CUPS (24 FL OZ/750 ML)

6 Tbsp (3 oz/90 g) unsalted butter	1 cup (8 oz/250 g) sugar
1½ lb (750 g) apricots, pitted and chopped	1 Tbsp kosher salt
	Juice of 1 lemon

In a heavy sauté pan over medium heat, melt the butter. Add the apricots and cook, stirring often, until they begin to soften, about 5 minutes. Add the sugar, salt, lemon juice, and about ⅓ cup (3 fl oz/80 ml) water and continue to cook, stirring often, until the apricots break down and the mixture takes on a jamlike consistency, about 15 minutes. Let cool, transfer to 1 or more sterilized, tightly capped jars or other airtight containers, and refrigerate for up to 2 weeks.

To serve with Pork Rillette (page 57): garnish with fresh Thai basil, shiso, or tarragon.

STRAWBERRY JAM

MAKES ABOUT 3 CUPS (24 FL OZ/750 ML)

4 Tbsp (2 oz/60 g) unsalted butter	Grated zest and juice of 1 orange
2 lb (1kg) strawberries, stemmed and quartered	Juice of 1 lemon
1 cup (8 oz/250 g) sugar	1 tsp kosher salt

In a sauté pan over medium heat, melt the butter. Add the strawberries and cook until they begin to soften, about 5 minutes. Add the sugar, orange zest and juice, lemon juice, salt, and about ⅓ cup (3 fl oz/80 ml) water and continue to cook, stirring often, until the strawberries break down and the mixture takes on a chunky jamlike consistency, about 15 minutes. Let cool, transfer to 1 or more sterilized, tightly capped jars or other airtight containers, and refrigerate for up to 2 weeks.

To serve with Pork Rillette (page 57): garnish with fresh basil, pickled strawberries, and a sprinkle of Maldon salt.

CONCORD GRAPE SPREAD

MAKES ABOUT 3 CUPS (24 FL OZ/750 ML)

1½ lb (750 g) Concord grapes	1 cup (8 oz/250 g) sugar
6 Tbsp (3 oz/90 g) unsalted butter	Juice of 1 lemon
	1 Tbsp kosher salt

Separate the flesh of the grapes from the skins by squeezing the grapes over a heavy saucepan. Put the skins in a food processor and process until puréed. Place the pan with the grape flesh over medium heat and heat until the flesh begins to break down, about 10 minutes. Mash the flesh with the back of a spoon, then pass through a fine-mesh sieve placed over a clean heavy saucepan and discard the seeds.

Add the puréed skins, butter, sugar, lemon juice, and salt to the pan and place over medium heat. Cook, stirring often to prevent scorching, until the mixture thickens and gels nicely, about 20 minutes. Let cool, transfer to 1 or more sterilized, tightly capped jars or other airtight containers, and refrigerate for up to 2 weeks.

To serve with Pork Rillette (page 57): garnish with fresh tarragon and roasted peanuts.

CRANBERRY SPREAD

MAKES ABOUT 3 CUPS (24 FL OZ/750 ML)

6 Tbsp (3 oz/90 g) unsalted butter	Grated zest and juice of 1 orange
5 cups (20 oz/625 g) cranberries	Juice of 1 lemon
2 cups (1 lb/500 g) sugar, or as needed	1 Tbsp kosher salt

In a sauté pan over medium heat, melt the butter. Add the cranberries and cook until they begin to soften, about 15 minutes. Add the 2 cups sugar, orange zest and juice, lemon juice, salt, and about ⅓ cup (3 fl oz/80 ml) water and continue to cook, stirring often, until the cranberries break down and the mixture is jamlike, about 25 minutes. You may need to add a bit more sugar depending on the tartness of the cranberries. Let cool, transfer to 1 or more sterilized, tightly capped jars or other airtight containers, and refrigerate for up to 2 weeks.

To serve with Pork Rillette (page 57): garnish with fresh basil, flat-leaf parsley, and toasted hazelnuts.

PEAR COMPOTE

MAKES ABOUT 3 CUPS (24 FL OZ/750 ML)

½ cup (4 oz/125 g) unsalted butter

8 ripe pears, peeled, halved, cored, and chopped

1 cup (8 oz/250 g) sugar

Grated zest and juice of 1 lemon

3 Tbsp fresh orange juice

Pinch of ground cardamom

1 star anise pod

1 Tbsp kosher salt

Freshly ground pepper

In a sauté pan over medium heat, melt the butter. Add the pears and cook, stirring occasionally, until they begin to soften into a mush, about 15 minutes. Add the sugar, lemon zest and juice, orange juice, cardamom, star anise, salt, pepper to taste, and a splash of water and continue to cook, stirring often, until the mixture resembles a thick applesauce, about 15 minutes. Remove and discard the star anise pod. Let cool, transfer to 1 or more sterilized, tightly capped jars or other airtight containers, and refrigerate for up to 2 weeks.

To serve with Pork Rillette (page 57): garnish with pickled Tokyo turnips and fresh chives.

HOT CHILE JAM

MAKES ABOUT 1 PINT (16 FL OZ/500 ML)

2 lb (1 kg) habanero or Scotch bonnet chiles, stemmed

Extra-virgin olive oil for drizzling

2 cups (16 fl oz/500 ml) fresh orange juice

1 cup (8 fl oz/250 ml) rice vinegar

3 cups (1½ lb/750 g) sugar mixed with 2 Tbsp powdered pectin

Grated zest and juice of 1 lemon

Grated zest of 1 orange

1½ Tbsp kosher salt

In a food processor, blast the raw chiles to a pulp. Transfer them to a saucepan, add a drizzle of olive oil, place over medium heat, and allow the chiles to sweat for about 1 minute. Add the orange juice, vinegar, sugar, lemon zest and juice, orange zest, salt, and about 1 cup (8 fl oz/250 ml) water and continue to cook, stirring often, until reduced to a jamlike consistency, about 40 minutes. Let cool, transfer to 1 or more sterilized, tightly capped jars or other airtight containers, and refrigerate for up to 3 weeks. This jam is great on anything and everything that needs an extra kick.

SPICED CARAMEL SYRUP

MAKES ABOUT 1 CUP (8 FL OZ/250 ML)

1 cup (8 oz/250 g) sugar

Squeeze of fresh lemon juice

¼ tsp ground cinnamon

¼ tsp white pepper

In a saucepan, combine the sugar, lemon juice, and 1 cup (8 fl oz/250 ml) water and stir to moisten the sugar evenly. Place over medium heat and bring to a boil, stirring just until the sugar melts. Continue to cook without stirring until the syrup thickens and turns amber brown. Slowly pour in ½ cup (4 fl oz/125 ml) water; work carefully, as the mixture will bubble up vigorously. Stir with a heat-resistant rubber spatula until smooth, scraping down any sugar crystals from the pan sides. Add the cinnamon and pepper and simmer for 2 minutes. Remove from the heat and let cool. Use immediately, or transfer to an airtight container and refrigerate for up to 6 months.

BASIC PICKLING LIQUID

MAKES ABOUT 6 CUPS (48 FL OZ/1.5 L)

2 cups (16 fl oz/500 ml) rice vinegar

1 cup (8 oz/250 g) sugar

3 cloves garlic

2 bay leaves

1 Tbsp mustard seeds

1 Tbsp peppercorns, crushed

2 Tbsp kosher salt

For a sweet pickle:
1 cup (12 oz/375 g) honey

For a spicy pickle:
2 habanero chiles, smashed

Your choice of fun things to pickle

In a saucepan, combine the vinegar, sugar, garlic, bay leaves, mustard seeds, peppercorns, salt, and 4 cups (32 fl oz/1 l) water. If making a sweet pickle, add the honey; if making a spicy pickle, add the chiles. Place over medium-high heat and bring to a boil, stirring to dissolve the sugar. Adjust the heat and simmer for a few minutes.

Meanwhile, place your choice of 1 or more vegetables or fruits to pickle (see below) in heatproof sterilized jars or containers. Pour in the hot pickling liquid, submerging them completely. Let cool to room temperature, then cover tightly and refrigerate. The pickles will be ready to eat within 1 hour. They will keep for up to 4 weeks.

fun things TO PICKLE fennel slices, radish slices, whole or halved green beans, whole okra pods, Tokyo turnip slices, beet slices, Japanese cucumber slices, whole strawberries, pear slices, whole cranberries, chile slices, onion slices, carrots, asparagus, whole or sliced mushrooms

BASIC CHICKEN STOCK

MAKES ABOUT 2 QT (2 L)

2 lb (1 kg) chicken wings

2 large yellow onions, chopped

6 ribs celery, chopped

2 large carrots, peeled and chopped

6 whole cloves garlic, smashed

6 whole cloves

Preheat the oven to 450°F (230°C). Spread the chicken wings in a roasting pan and roast until the skin is golden brown, stirring once or twice, 25–30 minutes.

Transfer the roasted wings to a stockpot and add the onions, celery, carrots, garlic, cloves, and 3 qt (3 l) water. Place over medium-high heat and bring to a simmer. Reduce the heat to maintain a simmer and cook, skimming any foam as necessary, until you have a well-flavored stock, 1–2 hours.

Remove from the heat and strain through a fine-mesh sieve into a heatproof container. Let cool, skim off the fat from the surface, and use immediately. Alternatively, let cool, cover tightly, and refrigerate for up to 3 days or freeze for up to 2 months, then skim off the fat just before using.

BASIC VEAL STOCK

MAKES ABOUT 5 QT (5 L)

10 lb (5 kg) veal knuckle bones

½ cup (4 fl oz/125 ml) canola oil

2 large yellow onions, chopped

6 ribs celery, chopped

2 large carrots, peeled and chopped

1 cup (8 oz/250 g) tomato paste

A few bay leaves

10 peppercorns, crushed

Preheat the oven to 450°F (230°C). Spread the bones in a roasting pan and coat with the canola oil. Roast until they are a deep golden brown on all sides, 25–30 minutes. Add the onions, celery, and carrots to the pan, stir to mix, and return to the oven until the vegetables are caramelized, about 20 minutes longer. Add the tomato paste, give the mix a stir, and continue to roast until the tomato paste is rust colored, about 4 minutes longer.

Transfer the contents of the roasting pan to a large stockpot. Place the roasting pan on the stove top over medium heat, add a few splashes of water, and deglaze the pan, stirring to scrap up any browned bits from the pan bottom. Pour the pan juices into the stockpot and add the bay leaves, peppercorns, and about 8 qt (8 l) water, or as needed to cover the bones completely.

Bring to a simmer over medium-high heat, adjust the heat to maintain a simmer, and cook, skimming off the fat occasionally, for about 8 hours. Do not allow the stock to boil. If it begins to reduce too much, turn down the heat.

Remove from the heat and strain through a fine-mesh sieve into 1 or more heatproof containers. Let cool, skim off the fat from the surface, and use immediately. Alternatively, let cool, cover tightly, and refrigerate for up to 3 days or freeze for up to 2 months, then skim off the fat just before using.

VEAL DEMI-GLACE

MAKES ABOUT 2 QT (2 L)

4 Tbsp (2 oz/60 g) unsalted butter

2 shallots, sliced

3 cloves garlic, sliced

1 batch Basic Veal Stock

2 cups (16 fl oz/500 ml) good-quality red wine

1 cup (8 fl oz/250 ml) sherry

A few sprigs fresh thyme

Kosher salt

In a stockpot over medium heat, melt the butter. Add the shallots and garlic and sweat until translucent, 3–4 minutes. Add the stock, red wine, sherry, and thyme and bring to a simmer. Adjust the heat to maintain a simmer and cook until reduced by about two-thirds and the sauce coats the back of a spoon, about 1 hour.

Remove from the heat and strain through a fine-mesh sieve into 1 or more heatproof containers. Season with salt and use immediately. Alternatively, let cool, cover tightly, and refrigerate for up to 3 days or freeze for up to 2 months.

EMMA'S GO-TO TOOLS

When it comes to cooking, you are often only as good as your tools. One big difference between restaurant cooking and home cooking is the equipment. Here are some of the staples I have at both work and home that make life easier and food sexier.

Hands Your hands are hands down your most important tool. Take excellent care of them. Don't be afraid to get them dirty and play with your food. It's the only way you can really get to know it intimately.

Intuition and integrity These are the two most important internal tools a cook can possess. Far more valuable than knowing exact measurements or techniques, they can add a hell of a lot of soul to a dish.

Microplane, mandoline, "speed" peeler I heart the Microplane grater. It allows me to zest, grate, and flake my visions to reality. Never leave home without it. A mandoline is a great way to achieve uniform, paper-thin slices. What I mean by a speed peeler is one that allows you to peel with the utmost speed, because who wants to be standing around peeling all day? You've got better things to do. You can also make tasty ribbons and shavings of cheeses, vegetables, and other ingredients with a good peeler. Be careful and focused when using any of these tools: don't shave your fingers down to nubs or you won't be able to cook at all.

Table-top deep fryer This is an inexpensive device that will add invaluable tastiness to your food, because no one can deny that everything tastes better deep-fried.

Heavy-duty food processor, high-powered blender (Vita-Prep 3), immersion blender, food mill, tamis (drum sieve), chinois (conical sieve), fine-mesh sieve, cheesecloth, coffee filters All of these tools and appliances will be your best friends in creating smooth, luxurious, restaurant-quality sauces and purées.

Pasta sheeter, pasta cutter The sheeter makes cranking out beautiful thin sheets of pasta dough easy. Have two pasta cutters on hand, one wheel with a fluted edge and another with a straight edge.

Serrated knife, paring knife In addition to the set of razor-sharp high-quality knives I have in the kitchen, I also have some inexpensive serrated knives and paring knives in my tool drawer.

Tongs, wooden spoons, wooden spatula, heat-resistant rubber spatula, metal spatula, whisk These tools are extensions of your fingers. Buy ones that are sturdy and feel as comfortable in your hand as your fingers.

Torch This is indispensable for applying heat in a particular place on an ingredient, getting frozen things out of containers, melting a chocolate glaze just a touch so it shimmers on your cake, burning off arm hair, and relighting pilot lights.

Plastic quart and pint containers These are what take-out food often comes in and they happen to be fantastic for storing *mise-en-place* items in the refrigerator in an organized manner. We could build a castle out of these containers at Sorella.

Rondeau Wide, shallow, and heavy bottomed, this versatile pan is a great choice for ragù and other sauces and even risottos. I shop for pans like this and my baking sheets at restaurant-supply stores, where the stuff they stock is built to last.

PANTRY ITEMS

Here are a few of my go-to ingredients to keep on hand. Stock up with these so you can always turn out kick-ass food on the fly. And yes, quality matters.

Oils
- Extra-virgin olive, grapeseed, canola, assorted nut types

Vinegars
- Aged balsamic, red wine, white wine, sherry, cider

Citrus
- Lemons, oranges, limes

Pickles and jams

Stocks

Fats
- Duck, bacon

Bacon and other cured pork products

Salts
- Table, kosher, Maldon and other finishing salts

Nuts and seeds

Spices
- Black pepper, white pepper, fennel pollen, red pepper flakes

Hard cheeses
- Grana, Parmesan, pecorino, Manchego

Soft cheeses, spreads
- Goat, mascarpone, crème fraîche, cream cheese

Fresh herbs

Tabasco or other hot-pepper sauce

Jarred oil-packed fish
- Tuna, anchovies

Tomato products
- Tomato paste, San Marzano whole and crushed tomatoes

Grains and dried pasta
- Quinoa, farro, Carnaroli rice, spaghettini, fusilli, rigatoni

INDEX

ACKNOWLEDGMENTS

FROM EMMA I humbly dedicate this book to my teachers, past and present, who I continue to learn from everyday. To my father, George, who has taught me grace under fire. To my mother, Christine, who has taught me to approach life with compassion and kindness. To my partner in crime, Sarah, who has taught me to have the courage to continue on down the road less travelled and the will to succeed. To my rocks, Molly Nickerson and John Barker, for teaching me sheer perseverance and how to smile on the toughest of days. To all of the generous souls who have put forth effort into making Sorella the special place it is today. Most of all to my Grandpa, George Hearst Jr, without whom none of this would have been possible. Thank you for believing in the dream and giving me a chance to grow. I am forever grateful for the strength and confidence gained through the experiences in which my fears were looked in the eyes.

FROM SARAH To my father, who gave me my love for food, my sarcastic sense of humor, and my hard candy shell. To my mother, who gave me my looks, my lady-like-ness, and my sweet sensitive side. To my brother Jon, who taught me how to talk, and is the smartest man in my life. To my brother Matt, whose courage and ability to overcome challenges inspires me daily. To my little sister, Rachel, who has always looked up to me and given me the strive to be a better person, because she is the best person I know. To George Hearst III, who has taken me in as one of his own since the first time Emma introduced us. To Emma, my partner in all this, best friend, and heterosexual life mate, who saved me from giving up on New York, and taught me how to have a good time, all the time. To all the great industry people I have met along the way who help keep me sane through camaraderie. And finally, to Mr. Penguin, who gives me unconditional love and snuggles, and keeps all my secrets.

FROM EMMA & SARAH All the thanks to the Sorella family, past and present, for joining us on a hell of a journey, to Stephanie Peterson and Tovah Avigail Weingarten for making up our faces and hair so we didn't have to at all, to Thomas Kikis for wardrobe and his little steamer, to Anais & Dax for their kick-ass photography, to Alison Attenborough and Paige Hicks for food and prop styling, to Chris Sorensen for recipe testing and for being a good friend, to Gramercy Tavern, Mother's Ruin, Neta, and Ducks for all their hospitality, for this book and in general, to Ashley Deleon for training us, for this book and in general, and to Amy Baker, who has saved our muscles and joints from expensive surgeries through massage and healing.